MARVEL STUDIOS
THE OFFICIAL COOKBOOK

MARVEL STUDIOS

THE OFFICIAL COOKBOOK

RECIPES INSPIRED BY THE MARVEL CINEMATIC UNIVERSE

Recipes Developed by Jenn Fujikawa
Written by S. T. Bende
Additional Recipes Developed by Evi Aki

INSIGHT EDITIONS

SAN RAFAEL • LOS ANGELES • LONDON

CONTENTS

PHASE ONE

PHASE TWO

PHASE THREE

INTRODUCTION

Over the course of the Infinity Saga, the Marvel Cinematic Universe has crafted one epic, interconnected storyline across dozens of films and series—and captivated audiences across the globe. In adapting decades of Marvel Comics lore for the screen, the Marvel Cinematic Universe has taken moviegoers on an ongoing journey that is as emotionally moving as it is breathlessly thrilling.

Better known as the MCU, this daring creative enterprise introduced a new era of interwoven blockbuster filmmaking. The twenty-three films of Marvel Studios' Infinity Saga, which range from 2008's *Iron Man* to 2019's *Spider-Man: Far From Home,* introduce the world to an iconic team of Super Heroes who band together to become Earth's Mightiest Heroes. While squaring off against brutal bullies, vengeful robots, and Asgard's mischievous "loveable scamp," the Avengers must also grapple with the looming, extraterrestrial threat of Thanos—a powerful tyrant who seeks to gather the ancient Infinity Stones and use their collective power to wipe out half of all life in the universe.

This book focuses on the Infinity Saga—the three-phased arc comprised of a multitude of films, each of which weaves an integral part of the MCU's storytelling tapestry. Phase One introduced the team of Super Heroes that form the initial team of Avengers, while Phase Two further expanded the MCU's roster of characters, propelling the story into the cosmos. The Saga concluded with Phase Three, which brought Thanos' plan to fruition and tested the Avengers' mettle like never before.

Throughout the Infinity Saga, our heroes are met with all manner of evildoers, shocking revelations, and, quite interestingly, culinary curiosities. After the Avengers thwart an alien invasion in the Battle of New York, they decompress at a nearby shawarma joint. The magically powered Wanda Maximoff and the synthezoid called Vision bond over paprikash—or, at the very least, Vision's sorry attempt at the Sokovian dish. In *Avengers: Endgame*, Thanos is seen preparing a hearty soup, which most likely went uneaten after the Avengers struck the Mad Titan down. Indeed, the Infinity Saga is a story of found family and resilience against all odds—one that just so happens to feature a universe's worth of delicious meals.

Within this book, you will find a celebration of the food found within the Infinity Saga, from homages and on-screen eats to recipes inspired by the films' characters or themes. Broken into three chapters, one representing each of the saga's three phases, this cookbook serves up dishes to honor each of the MCU's films. With recipes worthy of any skill level—and engineered to please a multiverse of dietary preferences—*Marvel Studios: The Official Cookbook* ensures that any Marvel fan can gather at your table for a meal worthy of a Super Hero.

So, what are you waiting for?

Ingredients, assemble!

(Finally, as any MCU fan knows, be sure to stick around after the credits of this book . . .)

PHASE ONE

In the spirit of the Marvel Cinematic Universe, our culinary journey begins with the first phase of the Infinity Saga. Comprised of the movies released from 2008 to 2012, Phase One serves as an introduction to the MCU's roster of heroes, bringing each to life through a series of solo adventures before assembling them for the first time in *Marvel's The Avengers.*

Throughout Phase One, we're introduced to the Earth's Mightiest Heroes, beginning with Tony Stark, a billionaire who abandons weapons manufacturing, creates the Iron Man suit, and dedicates his life to being a Super Hero. Next, audiences met Bruce Banner, whose inadvertent overexposure to gamma rays causes the scientist to transform into the rage-filled Hulk. Marvel Studios then brought in the Asgardian God of Thunder, Thor, who is banished to Midgard (aka Earth) and learns that selflessness is the true key to worthiness. Next, the MCU took audiences to the 1940s, introducing Steve Rogers—a determined kid from Brooklyn who doesn't like bullies. Rogers undergoes an incredible transformation, becoming the super soldier Captain America without losing sight of who he is—not a perfect soldier, but a good man. Alongside Natasha Romanoff and Clint Barton, the Black Widow and Hawkeye, respectively, these heroes join together to become the team known as the Avengers.

The following recipes are a tribute to some of the greatest moments from the Avengers' initial adventures. Tony's cheeseburger craving is immortalized in the "I Am Iron Man" Cheeseburger, while Thor's enthusiasm for a certain Midgardian beverage is marked by "Another!" Coffee. Capsicles are a playful nod to the Star-Spangled Man with a Plan, while Smashed Potatoes offer the Green Guy a delightfully delicious moment to shine. Avengers (and chefs) . . . *Assemble!*

"I AM IRON MAN" CHEESEBURGER

PREP TIME
20 minutes

COOKING TIME
35 minutes

YIELD
1 serving

DIFFICULTY
Difficult

After a harrowing—and innovative—escape from captivity, the first thing Tony Stark wants to do is sink his teeth into his favorite food: an American cheeseburger. This super-sized twist on an old-fashioned classic is larger than life, just like Tony himself. Beef and pork are blended into two patties, which are topped with cheese and sandwiched between three airy buns. Roasted red peppers add a pop of crimson while a golden pineapple Arc Reactor powers up the entire burger. This hearty meal is sure to provide a welcome homecoming for any Super Hero.

FOR THE PINEAPPLE

2 teaspoons unsalted butter
2 pineapple rings
2 teaspoons light brown sugar
⅛ teaspoon kosher salt

FOR THE BACON

2 strips bacon
1 tablespoon Dijon mustard
1 teaspoon honey
⅛ teaspoon white pepper

FOR THE BURGER

3 ounces ground beef
2 ounces ground pork
1 teaspoon Worcestershire sauce
½ teaspoon onion powder
½ teaspoon oregano
½ teaspoon paprika
2 tablespoons unsalted butter
½ teaspoon kosher salt
¼ teaspoon black pepper
2 slices cheddar cheese
3 brioche buns, toasted and buttered

FOR THE TOPPINGS

4 iceberg lettuce leaves, divided
3 tablespoons roasted red peppers
2 tomato slices
2 slices red onion

TO COOK THE PINEAPPLE:

In a medium skillet over medium-high heat, melt the butter. Sprinkle the pineapple with brown sugar and salt on both sides. Add the pineapple to the skillet and cook for 1 to 2 minutes, until the sugar has caramelized. Set aside.

TO COOK THE BACON:

Wipe out the same skillet and over medium-high heat, add the bacon. Cook for 1 to 2 minutes. In a small bowl stir together the Dijon mustard, honey, and pepper. Brush onto the bacon and continue cooking for another 2 to 3 minutes on each side until the bacon is crispy. Set aside.

TO COOK THE BURGER:

In a medium bowl add the ground beef, ground pork, Worcestershire sauce, onion powder, oregano, and paprika. Mix until just combined. Divide into two patties.

In a large skillet over medium-high heat, melt the butter. Add the patties, and season with salt and pepper. Cook for 3 to 4 minutes. Flip and cook for 2 to 3 minutes. Top each patty with a slice of cheese. Cover the pan and let cook for 2 minutes more, until the cheese has melted.

TO ASSEMBLE THE INGREDIENTS:

To assemble, add half the lettuce, red peppers, tomatoes, and onions onto the bottom bun. Top with one patty and the second bottom bun. On top of that, add the remaining lettuce and roasted red peppers, one pineapple ring, the second patty, and the bacon. Add the top bun and use a skewer to place the second pineapple ring on top.

IRON MAN

PROOF THAT TONY STARK HAS A TART

When a gravely injured Tony Stark is trapped in a desert cave, he only has one shot at saving his own life by making a daring escape. With the help of a brilliant colleague, Tony has everything he needs to build his first Arc Reactor, the power source of his Iron Man suit. With a coconut custard core and a ring of crimson raspberries, this tart pays homage to Tony's cave-side creation and the color palette of his future Iron Man suit.

V

PREP TIME
30 minutes

COOKING TIME
20 minutes

YIELD
6 tarts

DIFFICULTY
Moderate

FOR THE CRUST

1½ cups crushed chocolate cookies

4 tablespoons unsalted butter, melted

½ teaspoon vanilla extract

FOR THE FILLING

4 large egg yolks, at room temperature

½ cup granulated sugar

3 tablespoons cornstarch

One 13.5-ounce can unsweetened coconut cream

2 teaspoons coconut extract

½ teaspoon vanilla extract

1 pint raspberries

TO MAKE THE CRUST:

Preheat the oven to 350°F. Prep six 4-inch tart pans with nonstick spray.

In a medium bowl, stir together crushed cookie crumbs, butter, and vanilla until combined. Press into the prepped tart pans.

Bake for 10 minutes, until firm. Let cool completely.

TO MAKE THE FILLING:

In a medium bowl whisk the egg yolks, sugar, and cornstarch. Set aside.

In a small saucepan over medium heat, bring the coconut cream to a low simmer.

Stir ⅓ of the hot coconut cream into the egg mixture to temper. Then slowly whisk the egg mixture into the remaining coconut cream, whisking constantly. Bring to a temperature of 185°F, then remove from heat. Stir in the coconut extract and vanilla.

Spoon the custard into the prepped tart shells, spreading evenly.

Space the raspberries around the edges.

Refrigerate until ready to serve, ideally in a cave, with a box of scraps nearby.

Marvel Studios' *Iron Man* (2008)

100 ml

THE INCREDIBLE HULK

SMASHED POTATOES

Hulk has a secret: He's always angry, which is what makes him such a formidable Avenger. That anger can be a force for incredible good—or in this case, incredible flavor! This recipe for Smashed Potatoes is inspired by the Green Guy's strength: Even though we recommend using a handheld mixer to break up boiled potatoes, we can imagine that Hulk would give these potatoes an enthusiastic SMASH!

GF, V

PREP TIME
20 minutes

COOKING TIME
15 minutes

YIELD
6 servings

DIFFICULTY
Moderate

FOR THE PESTO

1 cup fresh basil leaves

1 tablespoon pine nuts

2 garlic cloves

½ teaspoon kosher salt

¼ teaspoon black pepper

⅓ cup extra-virgin olive oil

¼ cup grated Parmesan cheese

FOR THE POTATOES

3 pounds large russet potatoes, peeled and cubed

½ cup unsalted butter

½ cup light sour cream

1 teaspoon kosher salt

½ teaspoon white pepper

TO MAKE THE PESTO:

In the base of a blender, add the basil leaves, pine nuts, garlic cloves, salt, and pepper. Blend on low and drizzle in the olive oil until combined. Add the Parmesan and blend until just combined. Set aside.

TO MAKE THE POTATOES:

Bring a large pot filled with water to a boil. Add the potatoes and boil for 15 minutes, until fork tender. Drain—do not rinse.

With a handheld mixer on low, break up the potatoes. Stir in the butter, sour cream, salt, and pepper.

Transfer to a serving bowl. Swirl in the pesto to serve.

Marvel's The Avengers (2012)

THE INCREDIBLE HULK

UNDERCOVER PIZZA

Bruce Banner, a renowned scientist, learned to hide a monumental secret—when provoked, Bruce turns into a massive, rage-filled Hulk with terrible, destructive tendencies, all thanks to an unfortunate overexposure to gamma radiation. Undercover Pizza offers a tasty nod to Bruce's secretive life . . . and might even be able to temper the volatile temperament of the almighty Hulk. Homemade dough is topped with pesto, cheese, and a bounty of in-*green*-dients—from spinach to arugula. Packed with iron and filled with flavor, Undercover Pizza is the perfect antidote to a stress-filled day. Just ask Bruce!

V

PREP TIME
2 hours

COOKING TIME
15 minutes

YIELD
10 servings

DIFFICULTY
Moderate

FOR THE DOUGH

1 cup warm water, 110°F

1 packet (2¼ teaspoons) active dry yeast

3 cups bread flour, plus more for dusting

2 tablespoons olive oil, plus more for brushing

1 tablespoon granulated sugar

½ teaspoon kosher salt

2 tablespoons cornmeal

FOR THE TOPPINGS

⅔ cup pesto (Smashed Potatoes, page 15)

8 ounces mini mozzarella balls, drained

2 cups fresh spinach

2 cups fresh arugula

2 tablespoons extra-virgin olive oil, plus more for brushing

1 tablespoon balsamic vinegar

¼ teaspoon kosher salt

¼ teaspoon black pepper

¼ cup shaved Parmesan cheese

TO MAKE THE DOUGH:

In the bowl of an electric mixer, add the warm water and sprinkle over the yeast. Let bloom for 10 minutes.

Fit the mixer with a dough hook, add flour, olive oil, sugar, and salt. Beat for roughly 4 minutes until the dough forms a ball.

Grease a large bowl with olive oil and place the dough inside, rolling to coat in oil. Cover with plastic wrap. Place in a warm area and let proof for 1½ hours until the dough doubles in size.

Turn out the dough onto a floured surface and knead slightly until smooth. Cover with a kitchen towel and let rest for 30 minutes.

TO MAKE THE PIZZA:

Preheat the oven to 425°F. Sprinkle a pizza pan with cornmeal.

Form the dough into a 12-inch circle. Move to the prepped pizza pan. Use a fork to poke the dough evenly, then brush with olive oil.

Spread pesto on the dough. Add the mozzarella and spinach. Bake for 15 to 17 minutes.

Top with arugula. Drizzle with olive oil and balsamic vinegar. Season with salt and pepper. Add shaved Parmesan cheese. Slice to serve.

IRON MAN 2

GIANT DONUT

When life gets too heavy for Tony Stark, he forlornly sits inside a store's rooftop giant donut sign. There, Tony proves to himself that there are very few problems that can't be solved—or at least forgotten for a while—with the help of a sugary pastry. This massive donut is an homage to Iron Man's moment of indulgence. With its pink frosting and sprinkles, it's guaranteed to lift anyone's spirits!

V

PREP TIME
2 hours, 15 minutes

COOKING TIME
10 minutes

YIELD
6 servings

DIFFICULTY
Moderate

FOR THE DONUT

1 cup whole milk, warmed to 110°F

1 packet (2¼ teaspoons) active dry yeast

6 tablespoons unsalted butter, melted

3½ cups all-purpose flour

½ cup granulated sugar

1 teaspoon cinnamon

½ teaspoon kosher salt

¼ teaspoon nutmeg

1 teaspoon vanilla extract

2 large eggs

4 cups vegetable oil, for frying

FOR THE ICING

2 cups confectioners' sugar

2 tablespoons whole milk

4 tablespoons unsalted butter, melted

½ teaspoon vanilla extract

2 to 3 drops pink food coloring

2 tablespoons sprinkles, for decorating

TO MAKE THE DONUT:

In the bowl of a stand mixer fitted with the dough hook, stir together the warmed milk, yeast, and butter. Let sit for 10 minutes until the yeast starts to bubble.

With the mixer on low, gradually add the flour, sugar, cinnamon, salt, nutmeg, vanilla, and eggs until just combined. With the speed on medium, knead dough for 4 to 5 minutes until smooth and elastic.

Place the dough into a large bowl greased with nonstick spray. Cover the bowl tightly with plastic wrap and let rise for 1½ hours, until doubled in size.

Punch down the dough. Remove from the bowl onto a lightly floured surface. Knead lightly. Use your hands to form a large round shape and place onto a piece of parchment. Use a biscuit cutter to cut a hole out of the center, set aside. Cover the large donut and the donut hole with a tea towel and let rise for another hour.

In a large Dutch oven, heat the oil over medium-high heat to 350°F.

Carefully place the donut and the donut hole separately into the oil and fry, basting the top of both. Fry for 5 minutes. Gently turn over and fry for 4 minutes more, until golden brown. Let drain on a wire rack.

TO MAKE THE ICING:

In a medium bowl, whisk together the confectioners' sugar, milk, butter, and vanilla. Stir in the pink food coloring, until combined.

Pour the pink icing evenly onto the donut. Add the sprinkles, to decorate.

IRON MAN 2

STRAWBERRY ROSES

GF, V

PREP TIME
20 minutes

COOKING TIME
N/A

YIELD
4 servings

DIFFICULTY
Easy

When Tony Stark tries (and fails) to apologize to Pepper Potts, he arrives bearing gifts of strawberries. No doubt Pepper would have preferred flowers, or literally *any other gift*—as strawberries are the only thing in the world that she happens to be allergic to. A tongue-in-cheek tribute to Tony's grave misstep, these carefully carved Strawberry Roses are paired with sweetened sour cream to make a delightful dipping sauce. Aesthetically pleasing and exquisitely enticing, Strawberry Roses are the perfect way of saying *thank you* or *I'm sorry* . . . depending on the circumstance.

INGREDIENTS

1 quart strawberries, washed and dried

8 ounces sour cream

1 tablespoon confectioners' sugar

½ teaspoon ground cinnamon

2 tablespoons light brown sugar

With a paring knife, cut off one strawberry stem. Place the flat side down with the point up. Make four small, vertical cuts at the halfway point from the tip to the base of the strawberry. Do not cut all the way through.

Just above those slices, make a vertical cut between each one, again being careful not to cut all the way through.

At the tip, cut a small piece out of the center by making a vertical cut at the tip and cutting while rotating the strawberry counterclockwise.

Gently fan the petals out. Repeat with the remaining strawberries.

In a medium bowl, stir together the sour cream, confectioners' sugar, and cinnamon. Sprinkle the brown sugar on top. Serve as a dip with the strawberry roses.

"DID YOU BRING ME STRAWBERRIES? DID YOU KNOW THAT THERE'S ONLY ONE THING ON EARTH THAT I'M ALLERGIC TO?"

– PEPPER POTTS

"ALLERGIC TO. STRAWBERRIES."

– TONY STARK

IRON MAN 2

SMOKED SALMON CARPACCIO

Justin Hammer pulls out all the stops when trying to convince Ivan Vanko to help him take down Tony Stark. He serves the formerly incarcerated, whip-wielding physicist a meal that includes salmon carpaccio, organic ice cream, and an offer to become his benefactor—though all Vanko really wants is to be reunited with his beloved bird. Smoked Salmon Carpaccio draws on the shared meal of Iron Man's adversaries, serving up a citrus-flavored smoked salmon and capers. It's perfect for sharing with friends, family, new business partners, or avian acquaintances.

GF

PREP TIME
2 hours

COOKING TIME
3 minutes

YIELD
4 servings

DIFFICULTY
Easy

FOR THE SALMON

8 ounces smoked salmon, cut into 2-inch pieces

1 large grapefruit, peeled and sectioned

1 ½ tablespoons extra-virgin olive oil

1 tablespoon lemon juice

¼ cup fresh parsley, chopped

¼ teaspoon freshly ground black pepper

FOR THE CAPERS

1 cup vegetable oil

3 tablespoons capers, drained and dried

TO MAKE THE SALMON:

On a medium platter, arrange the smoked salmon and grapefruit segments.

Drizzle with olive oil. Squeeze the lemon juice. Sprinkle with parsley and season with pepper. Cover with plastic wrap. Place in the refrigerator for 2 hours.

TO MAKE THE CAPERS:

While the salmon is marinating, start the capers. In a small saucepan over medium-high heat, heat the oil to 350°F. Fry the capers for 2 to 3 minutes until golden brown. Let drain on a paper towel.

Sprinkle the capers over the salmon to serve.

> "SALMON CARPACCIO. ANYTHING YOU WANT HERE, WE GOT IT."
>
> – JUSTIN HAMMER

IRON MAN 2

WATERMELON BLAST

GF, V

PREP TIME
10 minutes

COOKING TIME
N/A

YIELD
1 serving

DIFFICULTY
Easy

Tony Stark knows how to have a good time. When he throws a birthday party at his Malibu mansion, he invites an abundance of acquaintances and demonstrates his impressive marksmanship by using his Arc Reactor to target an airborne watermelon. Watermelon Blast is a treat that's every bit as dynamic—but a lot less messy—than its explosive counterpart. Frozen chunks of watermelon are blended with soda, kiwi, and honey and garnished with a slice of lime. It's a frosty beverage that's sure to please a crowd—no fireworks required.

INGREDIENTS

2 cups frozen watermelon

2 tablespoons lime juice

1 cup lemon-lime soda

1 kiwi, peeled and sliced

1 teaspoon honey

1 lime slice, for garnish

In a blender, add the frozen watermelon, lime juice, and lemon-lime soda. Blend until slushy.

In a tall glass, add the kiwi. Drizzle with honey.

Pour in the watermelon slush.

Serve with lime slice.

Marvel Studios' *Iron Man 2* (2010)

THOR

WORTHY CHOPS

The God of Thunder shares a close bond with his beloved hammer Mjolnir, which was forged in the heart of a dying star. Whosoever holds Mjolnir—if worthy—shall possess the power of Thor. This recipe allows you to prove your worth by summoning Mjolnir to pound pork chops into thin, tender strips. But should your kitchen be lacking in Asgardian hardware, a meat tenderizer is equally effective in shaping the chops into neatly flattened portions. Coated in breadcrumbs and fried in a shallow pan, these Worthy Chops are a feast fit for the gods.

PREP TIME
15 minutes

COOKING TIME
15 minutes

YIELD
2 servings

DIFFICULTY
Moderate

INGREDIENTS

2 boneless pork chops
½ cup all-purpose flour
1 teaspoon garlic powder
½ teaspoon kosher salt
¼ teaspoon black pepper
2 large eggs
½ cup breadcrumbs
2 tablespoons grated Parmesan cheese
1 tablespoon minced fresh parsley
½ teaspoon dried oregano
1 cup vegetable oil, for frying
Lemon slices, for serving

Place a piece of plastic wrap onto a clean surface. Place one pork chop on the wrap, then another piece of plastic wrap on top. Use a mallet to pound out the pork chop to ⅛-inch thickness. Repeat with the second pork chop.

Set up a dredge station with three shallow dishes. Combine the flour, garlic powder, salt, and pepper in the first dish. Whisk the eggs in the second dish. Stir the breadcrumbs, Parmesan cheese, parsley, and oregano together in the third dish.

Pour the oil into a large skillet. Heat the oil over medium-high heat to 350°F.

Take the pork chops and dip into the flour mixture. Shake off the excess, then dip into the egg, and then into the breadcrumbs. Fry the chops for 3 to 4 minutes on each side, until golden brown.

Let drain on a wire rack for 5 minutes. Serve with lemon slices.

Marvel Studios' *Thor* (2011)

THOR

ASGARDIAN SQUASH SOUP

Thor Odinson is a god of action. After Frost Giants from Jotunheim break into Asgard's vault and steal the Casket of Ancient Winters, he begs his father to retaliate. When Odin refuses, Thor unleashes his fury by overturning a gourd-laden table. Asgardian Squash Soup imagines what might have been created from the squashed remains of Thor's rage. Roasted butternut squash is paired with cumin, sage, and thyme and simmered in a savory vegetable broth. It's a hearty, vitamin-rich dish that's sure to soothe even the fiercest of moods—Asgardian or otherwise.

GF, V, V+

PREP TIME
20 minutes

COOKING TIME
2 hours

YIELD
4 servings

DIFFICULTY
Moderate

FOR THE BUTTERNUT SQUASH

1 large butternut squash (about 4 cups)

1 tablespoon olive oil

½ teaspoon kosher salt

¼ teaspoon black pepper

FOR THE SOUP

1½ tablespoons olive oil

1 cup diced onion

2 stalks celery, diced

1 medium carrot, diced

1 garlic clove, minced

1 teaspoon ground cumin

1 teaspoon smoked paprika

1 teaspoon dried sage

1 teaspoon fresh thyme, plus more for garnish

32 ounces vegetable broth

1½ teaspoons kosher salt

¼ teaspoon black pepper

TO COOK THE BUTTERNUT SQUASH:

Preheat the oven to 400°F. Slice butternut squash in half and remove the seeds. Drizzle the squash halves with olive oil. Season with salt and pepper.

Place onto a baking sheet and bake for one hour. Peel the squash and place the flesh into a bowl. Set aside.

TO COOK THE SOUP:

In a large Dutch oven over medium-high heat, heat the olive oil and add the onion, celery, carrot, and garlic. Cook for 6 to 8 minutes, until softened.

Stir in the butternut squash, cumin, paprika, sage, and thyme. Cook for 2 minutes, until fragrant.

Add the vegetable broth. Bring to a boil.

Reduce heat to low. Cover and simmer for 15 minutes.

Use an immersion blender to puree until smooth.

Season with salt and pepper.

Garnish with thyme to serve.

Marvel Studios' *Thor* (2011)

THOR

"ANOTHER!" COFFEE

Asgardian customs aren't always appropriate here on Midgard. In this realm, pet stores don't typically stock horses, and unlike Thor upon first tasting coffee, we rarely smash drinkware on the ground . . . but you may consider doing just that after a sip of this sweetened latte! A cozy blend of coffee, honey, and steamed milk, this soothing drink is renowned across the Nine Realms as a delicacy that will have both gods and mortals eagerly crying out for *another*!

GF, V

PREP TIME
15 minutes

COOKING TIME
1 minute

YIELD
1 serving

DIFFICULTY
Easy

INGREDIENTS

3 ounces strong coffee

2 teaspoons honey

¼ teaspoon vanilla extract

6 ounces whole milk

⅛ teaspoon ground cinnamon

Stir the coffee, honey, and vanilla into a mug.

Pour the milk into a large microwave-safe cup and microwave for 45 seconds to 1 minute, or until an internal temperature thermometer reads 150°F. Place a frother in the mug and whisk for 30 seconds, until frothy.

Pour the milk over the coffee. Sprinkle with cinnamon and serve.

"THIS DRINK, I LIKE IT! . . . ANOTHER!"

– THOR

CAPTAIN AMERICA: THE FIRST AVENGER

CAP'S SHIELD COOKIES

Forged from vibranium, Captain America's nearly indestructible shield symbolizes his commitment to being a good man above being a perfect soldier. These cookies are fashioned in the image of Captain America's iconic shield, and even though this recipe doesn't require any vibranium, it is no less worthy of the First Avenger.

V

PREP TIME
30 minutes

COOKING TIME
10 minutes

YIELD
24 cookies

DIFFICULTY
Difficult

INGREDIENTS

3 cups all-purpose flour

1 teaspoon baking powder

¼ teaspoon kosher salt

1 cup (2 sticks) unsalted butter, softened

1 cup granulated sugar

1 large egg

1 teaspoon clear vanilla

1 teaspoon red food coloring

1 teaspoon blue food coloring

2 ounces white icing

In a medium bowl whisk the flour, baking powder, and salt. Set aside.

In the bowl of an electric mixer, cream the butter and sugar for 2 to 3 minutes until light and fluffy.

Stir in the egg and clear vanilla until just combined.

Slowly add in the dry ingredients until the dough just comes together.

Divide the dough in half. Add red food coloring to one half until fully incorporated. Set aside.

For the second half, divide that dough into two parts. Leave one part as is and set aside.

For the remaining part, add the blue food coloring until fully incorporated. Roll out into a log shape about 1 inch across.

Divide the red dough into two parts. Take one part and roll out to a rectangle. Place the blue log into the center, wrapping the red dough around it. Set aside.

Roll out the plain dough and repeat. Place the red and blue dough log into the center, wrapping the plain dough around it. Set aside once more.

Finally, roll out the remaining red dough, place the log into the center, then wrap around to complete. Place the dough log in the refrigerator for 20 minutes.

Preheat the oven to 350°F. Prep baking sheets with parchment.

Remove the dough log from the refrigerator. Slice into ¼-inch-thick rounds. Place onto the prepped baking sheets. Bake for 12 minutes. Let cool on a wire rack.

Use white icing to pipe a star into the center of each cookie. Once the icing is dry, the cookies are ready to serve.

CAPTAIN AMERICA: THE FIRST AVENGER

CAPSICLES

By 1945, everything was coming together for Steve Rogers. The Star-Spangled Man with a Plan was proudly serving his country, he'd freed his best friend Bucky from imprisonment, and he had a dance lined up with the brilliant and charming Peggy Carter. But everything changed when he made the selfless decision to divert a bomb-laden plane into icy Arctic waters. Steve foiled the evil plans of the Red Skull but sealed himself in ice in the process. Decades later, Tony Stark jokes that Steve might have missed a couple things doing time as a Capsicle. Even though the two heroes don't get along at first, even Tony would agree that these frosty treats serve up a sweet nod to Cap's time beneath the ice.

GF, V, V+

PREP TIME
15 minutes

FREEZING TIME
8 hours

YIELD
10 ice pops

DIFFICULTY
Easy

INGREDIENTS

Two 15-ounce cans coconut milk

1 cup granulated sugar

1½ tablespoons strawberry syrup

2 to 3 drops red food coloring

1½ tablespoons blue raspberry syrup

2 to 3 drops blue food coloring

SUPPLIES

10-serving ice pop mold

In a medium bowl, whisk together the coconut milk and sugar, until dissolved. Divide the mixture into three separate bowls.

Leave one bowl as is; this is the white layer.

In the second bowl, stir in the strawberry syrup and red food coloring. Set aside.

In the third bowl, stir in the blue raspberry syrup and blue food coloring. Set aside.

Pour the red mixture into the ice pop molds. Place into the freezer for two hours, until firm.

Pour the white mixture on top of the red. Add the sticks. Return to the freezer for another two hours, until firm.

Finally, pour the blue mixture on top. Then freeze for 2 to 4 hours or overnight, until frozen.

Remove from the ice pop molds to serve.

U.S.
U.S.

MODERN MARVELS

CAPTAIN AMERICA: THE FIRST AVENGER

STARK EXPO TREATS

In 1943, Howard Stark debuted the Stark Expo and, in the process, introduced the world to the scientific community's most ambitious new creations. While most of Stark's prototypes wouldn't be viable for years, one of the era's tastier creations was already a staple in kitchens across the country. Invented in 1939, rice cereal treats have since become a beloved favorite for anyone with a sweet tooth. Featuring red, white, and blue sprinkles stirred into a marshmallow mix, Stark Expo Treats offer a cheerful nod to what may well have been one of the Expo's most beloved snacks.

V

PREP TIME
10 minutes

COOKING TIME
2 minutes

YIELD
12 servings

DIFFICULTY
Easy

INGREDIENTS

2 tablespoons unsalted butter
5½ cups mini marshmallows
6 cups crispy rice cereal
2 tablespoons blue sprinkles
2 tablespoons red sprinkles

Prep a 9-by-13-inch pan with parchment sprayed with nonstick spray. Set aside.

In a large pot over low heat, combine the butter and marshmallows, stirring until melted.

Fold in the rice cereal and sprinkles, stirring until coated.

Spray a spatula with nonstick spray and press the mixture into the prepped pan. Let cool completely.

Cut into squares to serve.

MARVEL'S THE AVENGERS

CHOCOLATE-COVERED BLUEBERRIES

Tony Stark has his work cut out for him. Not only must he contend with the chaos-loving Loki, but he must do so while sequestered in a flying laboratory alongside the oft-volatile Bruce Banner and Loki's incomparably powerful scepter. As he works on unlocking the scepter's Mind Stone, Tony snacks on blueberries—and offers to share them with his colleagues. Chocolate-Covered Blueberries offer a sweet twist on Tony's preferred brain food. Coated with protein-packed peanut butter and antioxidant-rich chocolate, these fruity treats are the perfect thing to serve coworkers, study partners, or Earth's Mightiest Heroes.

GF, V

PREP TIME
30 minutes

COOKING TIME
10 minutes

YIELD
6 servings

DIFFICULTY
Easy

INGREDIENTS

1 ½ cups fresh blueberries

8 ounces chopped dark chocolate, divided

1 cup peanut butter

1 tablespoon coconut oil

1 teaspoon flaked sea salt

Wash and dry the blueberries. Set aside to dry completely.

Prep a muffin tin with parchment liners.

Add a heaping tablespoonful of blueberries into each liner. Set aside.

In a double boiler over medium-low heat, melt half the chocolate with the peanut butter and coconut oil. Stir to combine. Once melted, remove from heat and stir in the rest of the chocolate, until melted.

Pour the chocolate mixture over the blueberries, tapping the tin to make sure the blueberries are covered. Sprinkle with salt.

Place in the refrigerator for 20 minutes, or until solid.

Remove from the muffin tin and serve the blueberries on the liner.

"BLUEBERRY?"

– TONY STARK TO STEVE ROGERS

Marvel's The Avengers (2012)

MARVEL'S THE AVENGERS

TEAM SHAWARMA

Tony Stark doesn't exactly know what shawarma is, but he knows that he wants to try it. After an especially close call during the Battle of New York, his friends oblige him, and the Avengers gather around a table to share a meal in an utterly exhausted silence. Sure to delight any of Earth's Mightiest Heroes, this shawarma packs seasoned flank steak, tomato slices, and garlic sauce into a neatly wrapped flatbread, making it the perfect dish to serve at friendly gatherings, picnics, or victory celebrations in the aftermath of a thwarted alien invasion.

PREP TIME
20 minutes, plus an additional 4 hours for marinating

COOKING TIME
10 minutes

YIELD
4 servings

DIFFICULTY
Medium

FOR THE MARINATED STEAK

2 tablespoons lemon juice
2 tablespoons olive oil
3 garlic cloves, minced
2 teaspoons ground cardamom
2 teaspoons ground coriander
2 teaspoons ground cumin
2 teaspoons smoked paprika
1 teaspoon kosher salt
½ teaspoon black pepper
½ teaspoon cinnamon
½ teaspoon sumac
1½ pounds flank steak, sliced

FOR THE GARLIC SAUCE

1 cup cucumber, thinly sliced
½ cup Greek yogurt
½ cup sour cream
2 garlic cloves, minced
2 tablespoons lemon juice
½ teaspoon kosher salt

FOR THE SHAWARMA

1 tablespoon vegetable oil
4 pieces naan
1 medium tomato, thinly sliced

TO MAKE THE MARINATED STEAK:

In a small bowl whisk the lemon juice, olive oil, garlic, cardamom, coriander, cumin, paprika, salt, pepper, cinnamon, and sumac. Pour into a sealable bag along with the flank steak, tossing to coat. Refrigerate for four hours.

TO MAKE THE GARLIC SAUCE:

Squeeze the excess water out of the thinly sliced cucumber. Add to a small bowl along with the Greek yogurt, sour cream, garlic, lemon juice, and salt. Mix until combined. Refrigerate until ready to use.

TO MAKE THE SHAWARMA:

In a large skillet, heat the vegetable oil. Add the marinated beef and cook for 5 to 6 minutes, until medium rare.

Place each piece of naan onto a large piece of foil. Spread the cucumber garlic sauce onto one naan. Add a few slices of tomato. Top with ¼ of the beef, then roll tight, wrapping in the foil. Repeat with the remaining ingredients.

"LET'S JUST TAKE A DAY. HAVE YOU EVER TRIED SHAWARMA?"

– TONY STARK

MARVEL'S THE AVENGERS

THE SPACE SCONE

One of six Infinity Stones, the blue-hued Space Stone is encased within the cube-shaped Tesseract and grants its owner the ability to open portals for interstellar travel. With its immense influence over the physical dimension, the Space Stone is incredibly dangerous in the wrong hands, as it can bring about tremendous destruction. Luckily, with its fragrant aroma the other-worldly Space Scone—the first of this book's six Infinity Scones—is more likely to draw a crowd than an invading alien army. With hints of vanilla and a helping of blue-sugar glaze, the Space Scone is sure to unveil new worlds of flavor.

V

PREP TIME
20 minutes

COOKING TIME
15 minutes

YIELD
24 scones

DIFFICULTY
Easy

FOR THE SCONES

2¼ cups all-purpose flour

½ cup granulated sugar

1 tablespoon butterfly pea flower powder

1 tablespoon baking powder

¼ teaspoon kosher salt

½ cup unsalted butter, melted

1 large egg

1 cup heavy cream

2 teaspoons vanilla extract

FOR THE GLAZE

1 cup confectioners' sugar

1 teaspoon butterfly pea flower powder

2 tablespoons whole milk

½ teaspoon almond extract

TO MAKE THE SCONES:

In a large bowl whisk together the flour, sugar, butterfly pea flower powder, baking powder, and salt.

Make a well in the center of the dry ingredients and stir in the butter, egg, heavy cream, and vanilla, until just combined. Refrigerate dough for 15 minutes.

Preheat the oven to 400°F. Prep baking sheets with parchment.

Use a 2-tablespoon scoop to form rounds. Place 2 inches apart onto the prepped baking sheets. Bake for 15 minutes. Transfer to a wire rack to cool.

TO MAKE THE GLAZE:

In a small bowl, whisk together the confectioners' sugar, butterfly pea flower powder, milk, and almond extract. Drizzle over scones. For best results, drizzle in thick, straight lines back and forth across the scones. Once the icing has set, the scones are ready to serve.

Marvel's The Avengers (2012)

PHASE TWO

With releases that spanned from 2013 to 2015, Phase Two expanded the Marvel Cinematic Universe, deepening its tonal palette by venturing into decidedly darker territory. From Thor's battle with the Dark Elf Malekith for control of the highly destructive Aether to Captain America's confrontation with a ghost from his past, the Avengers face down seemingly insurmountable challenges. But through it all, the Marvel Cinematic Universe never lost sight of its infectious sense of fun and endless possibility. New characters like the ever-sunny Ant-Man injected the MCU with fresh humor, and with the introduction of the Guardians of the Galaxy, led by the dance-happy Star-Lord, the MCU launched itself into the cosmos.

The dishes offered up in this phase of recipes are every bit as expansive as the storylines themselves. From the Asgardian Ale that Thor bemusedly shares with a veteran played by Stan Lee to the Reality, Power, and Mind Scones that pay tribute to the all-powerful Infinity Stones, these recipes take key moments from the Infinity Saga and bring them into our own kitchens. With a Thai dish that introduces Captain America to some new flavors, and bacon-wrapped water chestnuts reminiscent of Pym Particles, the delicacies in this next section are truly unforgettable!

IRON MAN 3

HARLEY'S BAKED POTATOES

When Tony Stark flees his destroyed Malibu mansion, he crash-lands in Rose Hill, Tennessee, where he is accosted by young inventor Harley Keener, who wields a homemade potato gun. The wary Harley agrees to let Tony use his garage and supplies, and later, Tony sends Harley a Mark II Potato Gun. It proves to be an impressive upgrade and becomes a lasting symbol of the inventors' freshly forged friendship. This recipe pays a tasty tribute to that connection—packed with bacon, sour cream, and avocado, this is a great dish to share with budding geniuses and new friends.

GF

PREP TIME
10 minutes

COOKING TIME
45 minutes

YIELD
4 servings

DIFFICULTY
Easy

INGREDIENTS

4 large russet potatoes

2 tablespoons olive oil

1 garlic clove, minced

1 teaspoon kosher salt

4 tablespoons unsalted butter

½ cup shredded cheddar cheese

½ cup shredded pepper jack cheese

4 bacon slices, cooked and crumbled

1 avocado, sliced

1 medium tomato, diced

¼ cup sour cream

1 tablespoon everything bagel seasoning

Preheat the oven to 400°F. Prep a baking sheet with parchment.

Wash and dry the potatoes. Use a fork to prick the skin all over.

In a small bowl, stir together the olive oil and garlic. Rub onto the potatoes. Sprinkle with salt.

Place the potatoes onto the prepped baking sheet and bake for 45 minutes, until fork-tender.

Slice open the tops of the potatoes and add 1 tablespoon of butter to each one. Fluff the inside of each potato with a fork, until butter has melted.

Top each potato cheddar cheese, pepper jack cheese, bacon, sliced avocado, tomato, and sour cream. Sprinkle one quarter of the everything bagel seasoning on each potato and serve.

Marvel Studios' *Iron Man 3* (2013)

IRON MAN 3

GLUTEN-FREE WAFFLES

GF, V

PREP TIME
10 minutes

COOKING TIME
5 minutes

YIELD
4 servings

DIFFICULTY
Easy

Tony Stark meets a lot of people. From business engagements to red carpet events, his calendar is consistently packed. And while he fails to recall meeting Maya Hansen—a woman whose Extremis research is wreaking havoc on her unwitting test subjects—he tells the genetic biologist not to take it personally. After all, he doesn't even remember the gluten-free waffles he ate for breakfast. This recipe pays tribute to JARVIS' cheeky reminder to his boss. Made from mochiko flour and buttermilk, and sweetened with fresh blueberries, Gluten-Free Waffles make for a thoroughly memorable meal—one that's perfect for sharing with friends both old and new!

INGREDIENTS

2 cups mochiko flour

3 tablespoons granulated sugar

2 teaspoons baking powder

½ teaspoon ground cinnamon

⅛ teaspoon ground nutmeg

¼ teaspoon salt

2 cups buttermilk

1 large egg, beaten

1 teaspoon vanilla extract

2 tablespoons unsalted butter, melted

1½ cups blueberries

Prep waffle maker according to the manufacturer's directions.

In a large bowl, whisk together the mochiko flour, sugar, baking powder, cinnamon, nutmeg, and salt.

Make a well in the center of the dry ingredients and add the buttermilk, egg, vanilla, and butter. Stir until just combined.

Fold in the blueberries.

Pour batter into the waffle maker and cook until crispy and golden brown.

"DON'T TAKE IT PERSONALLY. I DON'T REMEMBER WHAT I HAD FOR BREAKFAST."

– TONY STARK

"GLUTEN-FREE WAFFLES, SIR."

– JARVIS

Marvel Studios' *Iron Man 3* (2013)

THOR: THE DARK WORLD

NINE REALMS STEW

In *Thor: The Dark World*, Asgard anxiously awaits the Convergence—the event when the Nine Realms align . . . and the boundaries between the worlds all but disappear. Nine Realms Stew is a hearty comfort food that would help gods and mortals alike get through such a destabilizing time. Fresh vegetables are simmered in broth, coconut milk, and a savory curry paste before being garnished with cashews and raisins. It's ideal for serving on cold nights, snowy days, or any time the alignment of worlds approaches. *Takk for maten*!

GF, V, V+

PREP TIME
30 minutes

COOKING TIME
45 minutes

YIELD
6 servings

DIFFICULTY
Difficult

FOR THE CURRY PASTE

1 teaspoon turmeric

1 teaspoon cumin seeds

1 teaspoon coriander seeds

¼ teaspoon ground cloves

2 tablespoon olive oil

1 medium onion, diced

1 large tomato, diced

¼ cup cashews

1 cup water

FOR THE STEW

2 tablespoons olive oil

4 garlic cloves, minced

1 tablespoon minced fresh ginger

1 teaspoon dried cumin

1 teaspoon garam masala

1 teaspoon turmeric

1 teaspoon kosher salt

½ teaspoon ground coriander

One 14-ounce can coconut milk

1 cup vegetable broth

2 medium potatoes (about 1 cup), peeled and cut into 1-inch cubes

1 cup broccoli florets

1 cup cauliflower florets

1 cup carrots, peeled and cut into 1-inch cubes

½ cup corn

½ cup green beans, cut into 1-inch lengths

½ cup peas

FOR THE GARNISH

1 tablespoon olive oil

½ cup cashews

¼ cup golden raisins

Fresh cilantro

TO MAKE THE CURRY PASTE:

In a skillet over medium-high heat, add the turmeric, cumin, coriander, and cloves. Cook for 1 to 2 minutes, until fragrant.

Add the olive oil, onions, tomatoes, and cashews. Cook for 8 to 10 minutes, until the onions are translucent.

Transfer the onion mixture into the jar of a blender and add the water. Blend until smooth. Set aside.

TO MAKE THE STEW:

In a large Dutch oven over medium heat, heat the olive oil and add the garlic and ginger. Cook for 1 to 2 minutes until fragrant.

Stir in the curry paste, cumin, garam masala, turmeric, salt, and ground coriander. Cook for 1 to 2 minutes until fragrant.

Pour in the coconut milk and vegetable broth.

Add the potatoes, broccoli, cauliflower, carrots, corn, green beans, and peas. Bring to a boil.

Lower heat to medium low and simmer for 10 minutes, until potatoes are fork-tender.

TO MAKE THE GARNISH:

In a small pan over medium-high heat, warm the olive oil. Sauté the cashews and raisins for 2 minutes, until lightly toasted.

Spoon the stew into serving bowls. Sprinkle each serving with the roasted cashews and raisins and add fresh cilantro to serve.

THOR: THE DARK WORLD

SIF'S SLICED SALAD

A fierce warrior and an accomplished swordswoman, Lady Sif has bested foes ranging from Frost Giants to Dark Elves. Her blade can cut through nearly anything, making it an effective weapon against the toughest of armor, formidable enemies, and even platters of fruit! Sif's Sliced Salad serves up an array of colorful treats, arranged into a rainbow reminiscent of the Bifrost, Asgard's bridge between the realms. Featuring mango, pineapple, and neatly sliced peaches, this dish is worthy of serving to any warrior.

GF, V

PREP TIME
10 minutes

COOKING TIME
N/A

YIELD
6 servings

DIFFICULTY
Easy

INGREDIENTS

3 cups mango, peeled and diced
1½ cups blackberries
1½ cups raspberries
¼ cup crushed pineapple
2 cups sliced green apples
2 cups sliced peaches
2 tablespoons lime juice
1 tablespoon honey
1 sprig mint, for garnish

In a serving bowl, toss the mango, blackberries, raspberries, and crushed pineapple.

Arrange the apple and peach slices around the bowl.

Squeeze over the lime juice. Drizzle over the honey. Add mint, to serve.

Marvel Studios' *Thor: The Dark World* (2013)

THOR: THE DARK WORLD

THE REALITY SCONE

When astrophysicist Jane Foster discovers a mysterious portal in London, she travels to another realm, where she's inadvertently infected with the Aether—a fluid relic with the ability to manipulate matter. Ultimately, the Aether solidifies into the Reality Stone, one of six stones that are as powerful as they are sought after. The Reality Scone shares the brilliant, crimson coloring of the Infinity Stone for which it's named. With a chocolaty, red-velvet base and a cream cheese topping, this heavenly scone is sure to be every bit in demand as its all-powerful counterpart.

V

PREP TIME
20 minutes

COOKING TIME
15 minutes

YIELD
24 scones

DIFFICULTY
Easy

FOR THE SCONES

2½ cups all-purpose flour
2 tablespoons cocoa powder
½ cup granulated sugar
½ teaspoon baking powder
¼ teaspoon kosher salt
½ cup cold unsalted butter, cut into pieces
1 tablespoon vinegar
1 teaspoon baking soda
1 cup buttermilk
1 large egg, beaten
2 teaspoons vanilla extract
2 to 3 drops red food coloring

FOR THE ICING

4 ounces cream cheese, softened
2 tablespoons unsalted butter, softened
1½ cups confectioners' sugar
¼ teaspoon salt
2 tablespoons whole milk
½ teaspoon vanilla extract

TO MAKE THE SCONES:

In a large bowl, whisk together the flour, cocoa powder, sugar, baking powder, and salt.

Cut the butter into the flour mixture with a pastry cutter until it resembles coarse crumbs.

In a small bowl, stir together the vinegar and baking soda. Stir into the flour mixture along with the buttermilk, egg, vanilla, and red food coloring until just combined. Refrigerate dough for 15 minutes.

Preheat the oven to 400°F. Prep baking sheets with parchment.

Use a 2-tablespoon scoop to form rounds. Place 2 inches apart onto the prepped baking sheets. Bake for 15 minutes. Transfer to a wire rack to cool.

TO MAKE THE ICING:

In a small bowl, stir together the cream cheese, butter, confectioners' sugar, salt, milk, and vanilla. Spread generously onto the scones, and serve.

Marvel Studios' *Thor: The Dark World* (2013)

CAPTAIN AMERICA: THE WINTER SOLDIER

CHICKEN SATAY

After spending several decades frozen in ice, Steve Rogers has a lot to catch up on. He grabs a notebook and writes a list of some highlights to experience in his new, modern world. Listed among cultural touchstones such as the *Star Wars* films and disco music is Thai food. And while Cap's 1940s taste buds are probably calibrated for a lot of boiled foods, he'd be bound to love this recipe for a classic Chicken Satay. Marinated in coconut milk and spices and served alongside a tangy peanut sauce, these Thai skewers pack a flavorful punch—one that's every bit as strong as Cap himself.

GF

PREP TIME
4 hours, 30 minutes

COOKING TIME
10 minutes

YIELD
4 servings

DIFFICULTY
Moderate

FOR THE CHICKEN

8 wood skewers
½ cup coconut milk
1 tablespoon tamari
1 tablespoon rice vinegar
2 garlic cloves, minced
1 tablespoon curry powder
1 tablespoon granulated sugar
1 teaspoon minced ginger
1 teaspoon turmeric
1 teaspoon ground coriander
2 pounds boneless, skinless chicken breasts, cubed
1 teaspoon kosher salt
½ teaspoon black pepper
2 tablespoons olive oil

FOR THE SAUCE

⅓ cup smooth peanut butter
1 tablespoon light brown sugar
3 tablespoons tamari
2 tablespoons rice vinegar
1 tablespoon lime juice
2 teaspoons sesame oil

TO MAKE THE CHICKEN:

In a shallow dish, soak the wood skewers in water for 30 minutes.

In a medium bowl whisk together the coconut milk, tamari, rice vinegar, garlic, curry powder, granulated sugar, ginger, turmeric, and coriander.

Place the chicken into a sealable container and pour the marinade over it. Marinate for 4 hours.

TO MAKE THE SAUCE:

In a small bowl, whisk together the peanut butter, light brown sugar, tamari, rice vinegar, lime juice, and sesame oil. Set aside.

TO ASSEMBLE THE DISH:

Remove the chicken from and discard the marinade. Thread the chicken onto the soaked skewers. Season with the salt and pepper.

Brush the grill with olive oil and heat to medium high.

Place the skewers on the grill and cook for 15 to 20 minutes until the internal temperature is 165°F.

Serve with peanut sauce.

"I'LL PUT IT ON THE LIST."

– STEVE ROGERS

CAPTAIN AMERICA: THE WINTER SOLDIER

RED WINGS

GF

PREP TIME
10 minutes

COOKING TIME
45 minutes

YIELD
4 servings

DIFFICULTY
Moderate

Sam Wilson may be sweet at heart, but he can pack a punch when Steve Rogers calls him into action. As a trauma counselor for military veterans, Sam displays strength, honor, and commitment to service, qualities that are embodied in his equally heroic persona, the Falcon. Wearing a modified version of the flight harness and mechanical wings from his Air Force days, the Falcon plays a key role in exposing Hydra's evil plot. Sam had to steal his flight equipment in order to battle Hydra, and with these sweet and spicy wings, you may want to hold them close, lest anyone snatch them, too. With this recipe, baked chicken wings are tossed with a soy chili crisp sauce. They're sure to please anyone seated around your dinner table—just be sure to keep them out of Hydra's hands.

FOR THE CHICKEN

2 pounds chicken wings
2 tablespoons baking powder
1 teaspoon garlic powder
1 teaspoon onion powder
1 teaspoon hot smoked paprika
½ teaspoon kosher salt
½ teaspoon pepper

FOR THE SAUCE

1 tablespoon light brown sugar
1 tablespoon chili crisp
1 tablespoon rice vinegar
1 tablespoon tamari
1 garlic clove, minced

TO MAKE THE CHICKEN:

Preheat the oven to 400°F. Place a wire rack onto a baking sheet and grease with nonstick spray. Set aside.

In a large bowl, toss the chicken wings with the baking powder, garlic powder, onion powder, paprika, salt, and pepper. Place onto the prepped baking sheet. Bake for 45 minutes until cooked through.

TO MAKE THE SAUCE:

In a small bowl, combine the brown sugar, chili crisp, rice vinegar, tamari, and garlic. Brush the sauce onto the chicken wings.

Turn the oven to broil. Broil the wings for 1 minute until crispy.

Marvel Studios' *Captain America: The Winter Soldier* (2014)

"I AM GROOT" BREADSTICKS

I am Groot. I *am* Groot. I am Groot? We are Groot!*

***Translation:**

Loyal, brave, and utterly selfless, Groot's love for his fellow Guardians is always *perfectly* clear, even if we don't know what he's saying. Is there a tastier way to honor this Guardian's commitment to his comrades than by baking these buttery, cheesy breadsticks? Serve them at your next dance-off, and your friends are guaranteed to cheer in agreement: We are Groot!

V

PREP TIME
2 hours

COOKING TIME
20 minutes

YIELD
8 breadsticks

DIFFICULTY
Difficult

FOR THE DOUGH

1 cup whole milk, warmed to 110°F

1 packet (2¼ teaspoons) active dry yeast

4 tablespoons unsalted butter, melted

2 tablespoons granulated sugar

3 cups bread flour

1 teaspoon kosher salt

1 tablespoon olive oil, for greasing

FOR THE TOPPINGS

4 tablespoons unsalted butter, melted

1 tablespoon Parmesan cheese

½ teaspoon kosher salt

TO MAKE THE DOUGH:

In the bowl of a stand mixer fitted with the dough hook, stir together the milk, yeast, butter, and sugar. Let sit for 10 minutes until the yeast starts to bubble.

With the mixer on low, gradually add the flour and salt, until just combined. With the speed on medium, knead dough for 5 minutes until smooth and elastic.

Place the dough into a large bowl greased with olive oil. Cover tightly with plastic wrap. Let rise for 1½ hours until the dough has doubled in size.

Punch down the dough. On a lightly floured surface, knead for 1 to 2 minutes, then divide into 12 portions. Roll each piece into an 8-inch log, shaping into Groot's body. With a knife, cut one end to make the head shape, and use small pieces to create the arms.

Place 2 inches apart onto a parchment-lined baking sheet. Cover with a tea towel and let rise for another 30 minutes.

Preheat the oven to 350°F.

TO USE THE TOPPINGS:

Brush the dough with butter and sprinkle with Parmesan cheese and salt. Bake for 20 minutes until lightly browned.

Marvel Studios' *Guardians of the Galaxy* (2014)

WHAT A BUNCH OF DONUT HOLES

Star-Lord described his Guardians of the Galaxy as a bunch of losers—by which, of course, he means "folks who have lost stuff." And while others might describe the ragtag team a bit differently (and they most certainly have!), anyone who knows the Guardians knows their sometimes-hardened hearts are softened with a touch of sweetness—just like these donut holes! In What a Bunch of Donut Holes, homemade dough is rolled into spheres, dusted with cinnamon and sugar, and assembled into the symbol for Nova Corps—the intergalactic military branch of the Nova Empire. It's showtime, donut holes!

V

PREP TIME
25 minutes

COOKING TIME
10 minutes

YIELD
13 servings

DIFFICULTY
Moderate

INGREDIENTS

1 cup apple cider vinegar
3 cups all-purpose flour
1 ½ cups granulated sugar
1 tablespoon baking powder
1 teaspoon ground cinnamon
½ teaspoon allspice
½ teaspoon kosher salt
¼ teaspoon ground nutmeg
½ cup buttermilk
2 large eggs
1 tablespoon vanilla extract
4 cups vegetable oil, for frying
¾ cup granulated sugar
1 tablespoon ground cinnamon
13 chocolate-covered pretzel sticks, cut in half

In a large bowl, whisk the flour, sugar, baking powder, cinnamon, allspice, salt, and nutmeg. Set aside.

Make a well in the center of the dry ingredients and stir in the reduced apple cider, buttermilk, eggs, and vanilla.

Let the dough sit for 10 minutes.

While the dough is resting, make the topping. In a small bowl, combine the sugar and cinnamon, stirring to mix well. Set aside.

In a large Dutch oven, heat the oil to 350°F. Fry the donut holes in batches. Drop the dough by 1-inch rounds, one at a time, cooking for 3 to 4 minutes, until golden brown. Let drain slightly on a wire rack, then roll in the cinnamon sugar mixture to coat.

Use the halves of one chocolate-covered pretzel stick and three donut holes to form each Nova Corps symbol. Serve immediately.

"THEY CALL THEMSELVES THE GUARDIANS OF THE GALAXY."

– RHOMANN DEY

GUARDIANS OF THE GALAXY

THE POWER SCONE

Secreted away on the planet Morag, the world-destroying Power Stone is stolen by Star-Lord and eventually given to the Nova Corps for safekeeping. The ube-flavored Power Scone evokes the rich, purple hue of its namesake stone, serving up a teatime treat in the form of this subtly sweet pastry. With a sweet coconut glaze, the delectable Power Scone won't herald a planetary apocalypse, but it will leave you wanting seconds.

V

PREP TIME
20 minutes

COOKING TIME
15 minutes

YIELD
24 scones

DIFFICULTY
Easy

FOR THE SCONES

2½ cups all-purpose flour
½ cup granulated sugar
1 tablespoon baking powder
¼ teaspoon kosher salt
½ cup cold unsalted butter, cut into pieces
1 cup buttermilk
1 large egg, beaten
1 tablespoon ube extract

FOR THE ICING

1 cup confectioners' sugar
2 tablespoons whole milk
1 teaspoon coconut extract

TO MAKE THE SCONES:

In a large bowl whisk together the flour, sugar, baking powder, and salt.

Cut the butter into the flour mixture with a pastry cutter until it resembles coarse crumbs.

Stir in the buttermilk, egg, and ube extract until just combined. Refrigerate dough for 15 minutes.

Preheat the oven to 400°F. Prep baking sheets with parchment.

Use a 2-tablespoon scoop to form rounds. Place 2 inches apart onto the prepped baking sheets. Bake for 15 minutes. Transfer to a wire rack to cool.

TO MAKE THE ICING:

In a small bowl, stir together the confectioners' sugar, milk, and coconut extract. Drizzle onto the scones to serve. For best results, drizzle in thick, straight lines back and forth across the scones.

Marvel Studios' *Guardians of the Galaxy* (2014)

AVENGERS: AGE OF ULTRON

ASGARDIAN ALE

When Thor describes his drink of choice—an ale that's best reserved for Asgardian warriors—an unimpressed army veteran, played by Marvel comics legend Stan Lee, insists that the God of Thunder should share his libation. However, Lee's character quickly discovers that Asgardian Ale is not for the faint of heart. This recipe for spiced cider offers a harmless homage to Thor's beloved beverage. Seasoned with nutmeg, this version of Asgardian Ale is a festive drink that will have you cheering in the words of the Norse gods themselves: *Skål*!

GF, V, V+

PREP TIME
5 minutes

COOKING TIME
15 minutes

YIELD
4 servings

DIFFICULTY
Easy

INGREDIENTS

4 cups apple cider

1 cinnamon stick

One 2-inch slice orange peel

½ teaspoon whole cloves

4 thin apple slices, for garnish

¼ teaspoon nutmeg, for garnish

In a large saucepan bring the apple cider, cinnamon stick, orange peel, and cloves to a boil.

Strain through a sieve to remove the cinnamon stick, orange peel, and cloves.

Pour into four mugs. Float the apple slices on top and sprinkle with nutmeg, to serve.

"THIS WAS AGED FOR A THOUSAND YEARS IN BARRELS BUILT FROM THE WRECK OF BRUNNHILDE'S FLEET. IT WAS NOT MEANT FOR MORTAL MEN."

– THOR

AVENGERS: AGE OF ULTRON

PIETRO'S SPEEDY EGGS

GF, V

PREP TIME
1 minute

COOKING TIME
1 minute

YIELD
1 serving

DIFFICULTY
Easy

Whether making his way around a room or saving the citizens of Sokovia, the speedy Pietro Maximoff is undoubtedly the fastest Avenger. In the spirit of Pietro's supersonic powers, hyper-efficient chefs can shave a few minutes off their morning routine with this savory egg dish. Pietro's Speedy Eggs combine a popular breakfast staple with parmesan cheese. Just pop the ingredients in a mug and cook them in the microwave for one minute to make a meal that's every bit as speedy as Pietro himself.

INGREDIENTS

1 large egg

1 tablespoon whole milk

⅛ teaspoon basil

⅛ teaspoon garlic powder

½ teaspoon Parmesan cheese

⅛ teaspoon kosher salt

⅛ teaspoon black pepper

½ teaspoon diced chives

Crack the egg into a mug. Add the milk and whisk for 20 seconds, until light in color. Stir in the basil and garlic powder.

Place into the microwave on high and cook for 30 seconds. Stir, then return to the microwave for another 30 seconds.

Season with Parmesan cheese, salt, and pepper. Top with chives to serve.

Marvel Studios' *Avengers: Age of Ultron* (2015)

ЕКСПРЕСНО БРЗО
ПОПРАВЉАМО ЦИПЕЛЕ
ОБУЋАРСКА РАДЊА
20%
ПРОМЕНЕ НА КОЖИ
СУПЕР
ПОПУСТИ

THE MIND SCONE

An Infinity Stone that grants the ability to manipulate the minds of others, the Mind Stone is eventually used by Tony Stark and Bruce Banner to create an all-new Avenger—the synthezoid named Vision. As the golden stone's culinary counterpart, the Mind Scone does *not* impart the ability to control thoughts, but it *does* pack a tremendous amount of flavor into one small pastry. With bursts of lemon and a sweet, citrusy glaze, the Mind Scone is bound to be snatched up in seconds.

V

PREP TIME
20 minutes

COOKING TIME
15 minutes

YIELD
24 scones

DIFFICULTY
Easy

FOR THE SCONES

½ cup granulated sugar
2 tablespoons lemon zest
2½ cups all-purpose flour
1 tablespoon baking powder
¼ teaspoon kosher salt
½ cup (1 stick) cold unsalted butter, cut into pieces
½ cup sour cream
¼ cup lemon juice
1 large egg, beaten
1 to 2 drops yellow food coloring

FOR THE ICING

1 cup confectioners' sugar
2 tablespoons lemon juice

TO MAKE THE SCONES:

In a small bowl, stir together the sugar and lemon zest. Set aside.

In a large bowl whisk together the flour, baking powder, and salt. Stir in the lemon-sugar mixture.

Cut the butter into the flour mixture with a pastry cutter until it resembles coarse crumbs.

Stir in the sour cream, lemon juice, egg, and yellow food coloring until just combined. Refrigerate dough for 15 minutes.

Preheat the oven to 400°F. Prep baking sheets with parchment greased with nonstick spray.

Use a 2-tablespoon scoop to form rounds. Place 2 inches apart onto the prepped baking sheets. Bake for 15 minutes. Transfer to a wire rack to cool.

TO MAKE THE ICING:

In a small bowl, stir together the confectioners' sugar and lemon juice. Drizzle onto the scones to serve. For best results, drizzle in thick, straight lines back and forth across the scones.

Marvel Studios' *Avengers: Age of Ultron* (2015)

ANT-MAN

ANT-SIZED TEA COOKIES

When Scott Lang wakes up in Hank Pym's home, he's shocked to find ants serving sugar cubes for his tea. As Hank explains, ants can lift objects that are fifty times their weight, and they might've been able to lug around these tiny cookies, too. A bite-sized treat bursting with color, these cookies might not be essential for saving the world, but they'd be great alongside a cup of tea.

V

PREP TIME
15 minutes

COOKING TIME
10 minutes

YIELD
60 cookies

DIFFICULTY
Easy

INGREDIENTS

1 ½ cups all-purpose flour
½ teaspoon baking powder
⅛ teaspoon kosher salt
½ cup unsalted butter, softened
½ cup confectioners' sugar
1 large egg
1 teaspoon vanilla extract
½ cup nonpareils

Preheat the oven to 350°F. Prep baking sheets with parchment paper.

In a large bowl whisk together the flour, baking powder, and salt.

In the bowl of an electric mixer, cream the butter and confectioners' sugar until light and fluffy. Stir in the egg and vanilla.

Gradually stir in the flour mixture until just combined.

Form small teaspoon-sized balls of dough. Roll in the nonpareils, then place onto the prepped baking sheet, 1 inch apart. Bake for 10 minutes. Let cool on a wire rack.

Marvel Studios' *Ant-Man* (2015)

THE SUNDAE OF OMNIPOTENCE

Before stepping into the suit of the astonishing Ant-Man, Scott Lang worked at Baskin-Robbins only to be fired when his (seemingly omnipotent) employer discovers his criminal past (Baskin-Robbins always finds out). After doing time serving up a variety of chilly treats, the menu's frosty confections are no doubt burned into Scott's brain. The Sundae of Omnipotence commemorates Scott's time behind the ice cream counter and his all-knowing boss. This mini-cinnamon-waffle sundae includes vanilla ice cream, chocolate sauce, and whipped cream. Perfectly portioned and topped with a cherry, this dessert allows you to bask in an abundance of sweet flavors that are absolutely unforgettable.

V

PREP TIME
15 minutes

COOKING TIME
5 minutes

YIELD
6 servings

DIFFICULTY
Easy

FOR THE WAFFLES

1 cup all-purpose flour

2 teaspoons baking powder

¼ teaspoon cinnamon

¼ teaspoon salt

½ cup whole milk

1 large egg, lightly beaten

1½ tablespoons maple syrup

½ teaspoon vanilla extract

1 tablespoon unsalted butter, melted

FOR THE SUNDAE

2 pints vanilla ice cream

½ cup chocolate sauce

1 cup whipped cream

¼ cup chopped walnuts

6 maraschino cherries

TO MAKE THE WAFFLES:

Prep a mini waffle maker according to the manufacturer's directions.

In a medium bowl, whisk together the flour, baking powder, cinnamon, and salt.

Make a well in the center of the dry ingredients and add the milk, egg, maple syrup, vanilla, and melted butter. Stir until just combined.

Pour batter by the tablespoon onto the waffle maker. Cook for 2 to 3 minutes until golden brown. Let cool, slightly.

TO ASSEMBLE THE SUNDAE:

Top each waffle with ice cream, chocolate sauce, whipped cream, and walnuts. Top with a cherry to serve.

Marvel Studios' *Ant-Man* (2015)

ANT-MAN

PYM PARTICLE BITES

While working as an agent of S.H.I.E.L.D. during the Cold War, Dr. Hank Pym develops the revolutionary Pym Particle. These subatomic particles with the ability to alter mass, density, and strength are then harnessed into specialized suits, which can shrink their wearer to the size of an ant. Just like their namesake, the savory Pym Particle Bites might look tiny, but their size should not be underestimated. Water chestnuts are wrapped in thick bacon slices, then baked to piquant perfection. Crisp, compact, and absolutely bursting with flavor, this recipe will yield a popular dish in any realm—quantum or otherwise.

GF

PREP TIME
10 minutes

COOKING TIME
30 minutes

YIELD
20 servings

DIFFICULTY
Easy

INGREDIENTS

1 pound bacon

One 8-ounce can whole water chestnuts, drained

½ cup ketchup

½ cup packed brown sugar

2 teaspoons tamari

½ teaspoon togarashi pepper

Wrap a slice of bacon around each water chestnut and secure with a toothpick.

Preheat the oven to 375°F. Place a wire rack onto a baking sheet.

In a large bowl, whisk the ketchup, brown sugar, and tamari. Toss the wrapped water chestnuts to coat.

Place onto the prepped pan. Sprinkle with togarashi pepper.

Bake for 15 minutes. Turn over and cook for another 15 minutes until bacon is crispy.

Marvel Studios' *Ant-Man* (2015)

PHASE THREE

Spanning the films released from 2016 to 2019, the third and final phase of the Infinity Saga introduced new nations and entirely new worlds, expanding the Marvel Cinematic Universe like never before. From the sorcerers of Kamar-Taj to the technologically advanced nation of Wakanda, with its awe-inspiring king and his loyal legion of Dora Milaje, this series of films took the MCU to new heights. However, just when the MCU's heroes seem invincible, an ideological battle between Captain America and Iron Man divides the Avengers and sets the stage for Thanos' terrifying takeover. Yet, even in the darkest moments of Phase Three, hope emerges: Carol Danvers, aka Captain Marvel, and her trusty Flerken enter the MCU. Although Earth's Mightiest Heroes experience unfathomable pain, Phase Three foregrounded the Avengers' greatest strengths: the heroes' commitment to the greater good and the found family they've built along the way.

The recipes of Phase Three celebrate the culmination of the Infinity Saga. From Wanda's Paprikash (a recipe that includes actual paprika, unlike Vision's valiant effort) to Roasted Yaro Root, we taste foods that the Avengers themselves might have enjoyed. And of course, no Marvel Studios movie would be complete without some teasers after the credits. A duo of post-credits recipes—based on the Marvel Television series, *Loki*—offers a peek inside the Time Variance Authority, featuring appearances by Miss Minutes Cookies and a fresh Mobius Salad, complete with three variants! With recipes ranging from the buttery Flerken Nibbles to the Hulk's protein-packed breakfast burritos, this third phase of dishes offers something for everyone—whether you're keeping your meals earthbound, or taking your meals *higher, further, faster*!

CAPTAIN AMERICA: CIVIL WAR

WANDA'S PAPRIKASH

PREP TIME
30 minutes

COOKING TIME
1 hour

YIELD
6 servings

DIFFICULTY
Difficult

When Vision tries to lift Wanda's spirits by cooking her beloved paprikash, his culinary creation doesn't quite hit the mark. In his defense, he's never actually eaten anything, so he isn't the best at sourcing ingredients. When it comes to true paprikash, the Sokovian dish, inspired by the classic Hungarian dish of the same name, calls for both sweet and hot paprika, and it is served over traditional nokedli—dumplings made from eggs, water, flour, and thyme. Smoky, savory, and delightfully filling, Wanda's Paprikash is a tried-and-true comfort food that's sure to cheer up any Avenger.

FOR THE CHICKEN

3 pounds chicken thighs and drumsticks

1½ teaspoons kosher salt

1 teaspoon black pepper

2 tablespoons unsalted butter

1 tablespoon olive oil

1 large onion, sliced

3 garlic cloves, minced

2 tablespoons sweet Hungarian paprika

1 tablespoon hot Hungarian paprika

12 ounces chicken broth

2 tablespoons cornstarch

1 cup sour cream

1 tablespoon chopped parsley, for garnish

FOR THE DUMPLINGS

2 large eggs

¾ cup water

1¾ cups all-purpose flour

½ teaspoon dried thyme

½ teaspoon kosher salt

TO MAKE THE CHICKEN:

Season the chicken with the salt and pepper. Set aside.

In a Dutch oven over medium-high heat, add the butter and olive oil and sear the chicken for 5 minutes on each side until browned. Remove to a plate and set aside.

Add the onions and garlic and cook for 3 minutes until soft. Turn heat to low and stir in the sweet Hungarian paprika and hot Hungarian paprika.

Whisk in the chicken broth, then add the chicken back to the pot, nestling it into the liquid. Cover and cook for 45 minutes.

TO MAKE THE DUMPLINGS:

While the chicken is cooking, in a large bowl whisk the eggs and water. Stir in the flour, thyme, and salt until just combined. Let sit for 10 minutes.

Bring a large pot of salted water to a boil. Use a teaspoon to drop small pieces of dough into the water, about one dozen at a time. Boil the dumplings for 4 to 5 minutes. Drain and place on a serving plate.

TO ASSEMBLE THE DISH:

Remove the chicken from the pot and place on top of the dumplings. In a small bowl, stir together the cornstarch and ½ cup of broth. Add the mixture back to the pot and bring to a boil for 1 minute, just until thickened. Stir in the sour cream.

Pour the sauce over the chicken and sprinkle with parsley to serve.

"I DON'T KNOW WHAT'S IN THIS, BUT IT IS NOT PAPRIKA."

– WANDA MAXIMOFF

DOES ANYONE HAVE ANY ORANGE SORBET?

When Captain America faces off against Iron Man at an airport in Germany, the renegade Avenger is counting on Ant-Man to provide a big distraction. The size-altering Pym Particles can allow Scott to grow to sixty-five feet in height but he's only ever done it once . . . in a lab . . . and then he passed out. Nonetheless, Scott sizes up to face down his opponents, and when it's all over, he finds himself battered, exhausted, and desperately craving orange slices. This tangy recipe serves up a refreshingly frosty treat that would have been just what the oversized hero ordered.

GF, V, V+

PREP TIME
15 minutes, plus an additional 1.5 hours cooling time

FREEZING TIME
4 hours

YIELD
4 servings

DIFFICULTY
Easy

INGREDIENTS

1½ cups water

⅔ cup granulated sugar

3 oranges, equal to 1 cup fresh orange juice

2 tablespoons fresh lemon juice

Mint leaves, for garnish

In a saucepan over medium-high heat, bring the water and sugar to a boil. Turn off the heat and let cool completely.

Slice the oranges in half, squeeze and reserve the juice. Place orange rinds aside, upside down on a towel to dry.

In a bowl, stir together the reserved orange juice, lemon juice, and cooled simple syrup mixture. Pour into a loaf pan and freeze for 4 hours, stirring every hour.

Scoop the sorbet into the hollowed-out orange rinds to serve. Add a mint leaf to garnish.

"DOES ANYONE HAVE ANY ORANGE SLICES?"

– ANT-MAN

Marvel Studios' *Captain America: Civil War* (2016)

CAPTAIN AMERICA: CIVIL WAR

MAY'S WALNUT DATE LOAF

Tony Stark has a hard time believing that May Parker is someone's aunt. Not only is she singlehandedly raising her nephew Peter while carving out time to serve her community, but she's an impressively gifted host to boot. May's Walnut Date Loaf combines dates, walnuts, and brown sugar to create a nutty bread that's great to keep on hand for unexpected guests.

V

PREP TIME
40 minutes

COOKING TIME
45 minutes

YIELD
1 loaf or
8 servings

DIFFICULTY
Easy

INGREDIENTS

1½ cups chopped dates
¾ cup packed light brown sugar
1 teaspoon baking soda
4 tablespoons unsalted butter, softened
1 cup boiling water
1 large egg
1 teaspoon vanilla extract
2 cups all-purpose flour
1 teaspoon baking soda
½ teaspoon cinnamon
½ teaspoon kosher salt
¼ teaspoon nutmeg
¾ cup chopped walnuts

Preheat the oven to 350°F. Grease a loaf pan with nonstick spray.

In a large bowl, stir together the dates, brown sugar, baking soda, and butter. Pour the boiling water over the date mixture. Let sit for 30 minutes.

Stir in the egg and vanilla until just combined.

Stir in the flour, baking soda, cinnamon, salt, and nutmeg, stirring until smooth. Fold in the walnuts.

Pour the batter into the prepped pan. Bake for 45 minutes until an inserted toothpick comes out clean. Let cool completely on a wire rack.

Slice and serve.

"THIS WALNUT DATE LOAF IS EXCEPTIONAL."

– TONY STARK

DOCTOR STRANGE

EGGS OF AGAMATTO

Guarded by the Masters of the Mystic Arts, the Eye of Agamotto is a magical object that houses the Time Stone, which grants power over all things temporal. With their green centers and crispy, fried onion garnish, these Eggs of Agamotto bear a striking resemblance to the most important piece of Doctor Strange's getup. They make for a protein-rich way to kick off the day—an ideal start for anyone seeking to master the mystic arts.

V

PREP TIME
10 minutes

COOKING TIME
10 minutes

YIELD
12 servings

DIFFICULTY
Easy

INGREDIENTS

6 large eggs
3 tablespoons mayonnaise
1 tablespoon sweet pickle relish
2 teaspoons Dijon mustard
¼ teaspoon paprika
¼ teaspoon seasoned salt
¼ teaspoon turmeric
⅛ teaspoon celery seed
⅛ teaspoon black pepper
12 green Spanish olives
¼ cup fried onions

Place the eggs in a large saucepan and cover them by 1 to 2 inches with water. Turn on the heat to medium high and bring to a boil.

Turn off the heat, cover with a lid, and let sit for 10 to 12 minutes.

Place the eggs in an ice bath and let cool completely.

Peel and slice the eggs in half. Set aside the whites and place the yolks into a large bowl.

Add the mayonnaise, relish, Dijon mustard, paprika, seasoned salt, turmeric, celery seed, and pepper to the yolks. Stir until just combined. Place into a piping bag and pipe into the egg whites, filling the center of the eggs.

Place one Spanish olive into the center of each piped. Place the fried onions on top of the eggs to garnish.

Refrigerate until ready to serve.

Marvel Studios' *Doctor Strange* (2016)

DOCTOR STRANGE

THE TIME SCONE

The emerald hue of the fifth Infinity Scone pays homage to the stone ensconced within the Eye of Agamotto: the Time Stone, which Doctor Strange uses to trap the evil Dark Dimension entity Dormammu in a torturous time loop. With notes of vanilla, this pandan-flavored pastry is so good you'll wish you were trapped in a scone-filled time loop of your own! Sweet, buttery, and delectably crumbly, the Time Scone is one treat any lucky brunch guest would happily bargain for.

V

PREP TIME
15 minutes

COOKING TIME
15 minutes

YIELD
24 scones

DIFFICULTY
Easy

INGREDIENTS

2½ cups all-purpose flour
½ cup light brown sugar
1 tablespoon baking powder
¼ teaspoon kosher salt
6 tablespoons cold unsalted butter, cut into pieces
½ cup cream cheese, softened
1 cup whole milk
1 large egg, beaten
1½ teaspoons pandan extract
½ teaspoon vanilla extract
¼ cup confectioners' sugar, for dusting

In a large bowl whisk together the flour, brown sugar, baking powder, and salt.

Cut the butter into the flour mixture with a pastry cutter until it resembles coarse crumbs.

Stir in the cream cheese, milk, egg, pandan extract, and vanilla until just combined. Refrigerate dough for 15 minutes.

Preheat the oven to 400°F. Prep baking sheets with parchment.

Use a 2-tablespoon scoop to form rounds. Place 2 inches apart onto the prepped baking sheets. Bake for 15 minutes. Transfer to a wire rack to cool.

Dust with confectioners' sugar and serve.

Marvel Studios' *Doctor Strange* (2016)

GUARDIANS OF THE GALAXY VOL. 2

ROASTED YARO ROOT

The colorful yaro root is a favorite snack of the Guardians of the Galaxy. Known for its gradated green skin and purple tufted end, the root is kept in a bowl on the Guardians' ship, the *Milano*, where the heroes wait for it to ripen. Despite her sister Gamora's warnings that the yaro root is not yet fit for consumption, Nebula steals a too-bitter bite. Luckily, the Earth-based version of this beloved cosmic staple is much tastier. Here, cubed sweet potatoes are baked with cinnamon and smoked paprika. Sweet and filling, Roasted Yaro Root won't heal any long-simmering resentment between estranged siblings, but it will please any crowd on your starship.

GF, V, V+

PREP TIME
15 minutes

COOKING TIME
45 minutes

YIELD
6 servings

DIFFICULTY
Easy

INGREDIENTS

4 medium sweet potatoes, peeled and cubed

2 tablespoons olive oil

1 teaspoon cinnamon

1 teaspoon smoked paprika

1 teaspoon kosher salt

½ teaspoon black pepper

¼ cup brown sugar

2 teaspoons chopped fresh parsley

Preheat the oven to 400°F. Prep a baking sheet with parchment.

In a large bowl toss the sweet potatoes with the olive oil, cinnamon, paprika, salt, and pepper. Spread onto the parchment lined pan. Bake for 45 minutes.

Set oven to broil. Sprinkle the potatoes with the brown sugar. Broil for 2 to 3 minutes until caramelized.

Sprinkle with the parsley and serve.

"I'M HUNGRY. HAND ME SOME OF THAT YARO ROOT."

– NEBULA

"NO. IT'S NOT RIPE. AND I HATE YOU."

– GAMORA

GUARDIANS OF THE GALAXY VOL. 2

TRASH PANDA COOKIES

V

PREP TIME
20 minutes

COOKING TIME
15 minutes

YIELD
24 cookies

DIFFICULTY
Easy

Rocket might not know exactly what a raccoon is, but he knows he doesn't want to be called one. While arguing with his colleague, Peter Quill calls Rocket by his least-favorite title . . . then ups the ante and calls him a trash panda. Although Rocket is unimpressed, he might sing a different tune after taking a bite of these culinarily cacophonous cookies. Here a medley of chips (chocolate, butterscotch, *and* potato), pretzels, and oats are blended together in a delectable dough that's bound to bring even the most cantankerous colleagues together. Sweet, salty, and unapologetically wild, Trash Panda Cookies make for a truly Awesome Mix!

INGREDIENTS

2 cups all-purpose flour

½ cup oats

1 teaspoon baking soda

½ teaspoon kosher salt

1 cup (2 sticks) unsalted butter, softened

1 cup granulated sugar

¾ cup packed light brown sugar

2 teaspoons vanilla extract

2 large eggs

1 cup chocolate chips

1 cup butterscotch chips

1 cup chopped potato chips

1 cup chopped pretzels

Preheat the oven to 350°F and line baking sheets with parchment.

In a large bowl whisk together the flour, oats, baking soda, and salt. Set aside.

In the bowl of an electric mixer cream the butter, granulated sugar, and brown sugar. Add the vanilla and the eggs until combined.

Stir in the dry ingredients until the dough comes together.

Fold in the chocolate chips, butterscotch chips, potato chips, and pretzels.

Scoop 1-inch rounds of dough onto the prepped baking sheets, 2 inches apart.

Bake for 15 minutes, until browned and cooked through. Let cool on a wire rack.

"DON'T CALL ME A RACOON!"

– ROCKET

"I'M SORRY. I TOOK IT TOO FAR. I MEANT TRASH PANDA."

– PETER QUILL

"IS THAT BETTER?"

– ROCKET

"I DON'T KNOW."

– DRAX

GUARDIANS OF THE GALAXY VOL. 2

CELESTIALS PARFAIT

Ego is a godlike Celestial—a living planet capable of manifesting humanoid forms . . . and who also happens to be Peter Quill's father. The planet is home to a kaleidoscope of colors that reflect the varied elements of Ego's complex personality. Similarly, this vibrant Celestial Parfait exists in a burst of color. Brilliantly saturated jelly cubes are topped off with whipped cream and fresh fruit. Bright, tangy, and packed with sweetness, this flavorful dessert is truly out of this world.

GF

PREP TIME
5 hours

COOKING TIME
N/A

YIELD
8 servings

DIFFICULTY
Moderate

FOR THE BLUE GELATIN

3 ounces blue raspberry gelatin

1 cup boiling water

FOR THE GREEN GELATIN

3 ounces lime gelatin

1 cup boiling water

FOR THE ORANGE GELATIN

3 ounces orange gelatin

1 cup boiling water

FOR THE YELLOW GELATIN

3 ounces lemon gelatin

1 cup boiling water

FOR THE TOPPING

2 cups whipped cream

½ cup blackberries

½ cup diced mango

8 rambutans

TO MAKE THE BLUE GELATIN:

In a medium bowl, dissolve the blue raspberry gelatin in the boiling water. Whisk until clear. Pour into a small container, and cover. Set aside.

TO MAKE THE GREEN GELATIN:

In a separate medium bowl, dissolve the lime gelatin in the boiling water. Whisk until clear. Pour into a separate small container, and cover.

TO MAKE THE ORANGE GELATIN:

In another separate medium bowl, dissolve the orange gelatin in the boiling water. Whisk until clear. Pour into a separate small container, and cover.

TO MAKE THE YELLOW GELATIN:

Finally, in a separate medium bowl, dissolve the lemon gelatin in the boiling water. Whisk until clear. Pour into a separate small container, and cover.

Refrigerate all the gelatins for 5 hours, or until solid.

TO ASSEMBLE THE DISH:

Once solid, cut gelatin into small cubes, toss together, and spoon a layer into parfait glasses. Then add a layer of whipped cream, and alternate layers, and finally top with fruit to serve.

Marvel Studios' *Guardians of the Galaxy Vol. 2* (2017)

GUARDIANS OF THE GALAXY VOL. 2

RAVAGER SALUTE CUPCAKES

The Ravagers—a band of intergalactic outlaws—convey their respect by pounding a single fist to the chest. The time-honored Ravager Salute is seen in greetings, farewells, and, in the case of Yondu Udonta, at a firework-filled funeral. Ravager Salute Cupcakes provide a colorful culinary tribute to everyone's favorite Ravager. Rainbow-hued batter is layered into cupcake liners, baked to perfection and topped with cream cheese frosting. Bright, festive, and altogether awesome, these treats will have you pounding your chest in tribute . . . and feeling just the slightest bit like Mary Poppins, y'all!

V

PREP TIME
30 minutes

COOKING TIME
15 minutes

YIELD
18 servings

DIFFICULTY
Moderate

FOR THE CUPCAKES

2½ cups sifted cake flour

2 teaspoons baking powder

¼ teaspoon kosher salt

¾ cup (1½ sticks) unsalted butter, softened

1¾ cups granulated sugar

3 large eggs

2 teaspoons vanilla extract

1 cup buttermilk

2 to 3 drops red food coloring

2 to 3 drops yellow food coloring

2 to 3 drops green food coloring

2 to 3 drops blue food coloring

2 to 3 drops purple food coloring

FOR THE FROSTING

8 ounces cream cheese, softened

½ cup (1 stick) unsalted butter, softened

1½ cups confectioners' sugar

1 teaspoon vanilla extract

¼ teaspoon kosher salt

⅓ cup heavy whipping cream

TO BAKE THE CUPCAKES:

Preheat oven to 350°F. Prep a cupcake pan with liners.

In a medium bowl whisk the flour, baking powder, and salt. Set aside.

In the bowl of an electric mixer, cream the butter and sugar until fluffy.

Add the eggs and vanilla.

Alternate adding the buttermilk and the dry ingredients until just combined.

Divide the batter equally into five bowls.

Add one color of food coloring to each bowl, stirring until incorporated.

Drop the colored batter by tablespoonfuls into the liners.

Bake for 15 to 17 minutes or until an inserted toothpick comes out clean. Let cool on a wire rack.

TO MAKE THE FROSTING:

In a large bowl with a hand mixer, combine the cream cheese, butter, confectioners' sugar, vanilla, and salt. Slowly add the heavy whipping cream and beat for 2 minutes until light and fluffy.

Frost the cooled cupcakes.

Marvel Studios' *Guardians of the Galaxy Vol. 2* (2017)

SPIDER-MAN: HOMECOMING

PETER'S BODEGA SANDWICH

With great power, there must also come a great appetite. As a frequent patron of Delmar's Deli-Grocery, Peter Parker, aka the friendly neighborhood Spider-Man, always orders the same thing: a number five with pickles, smushed down real flat. This sandwich is a nod to the web-head's favorite after-school meal, and it features two slices of tart rye bread loaded up with pastrami, Swiss cheese, caramelized onions, mustard, and of course, pickles. Pressed down just like Peter would want, this sandwich is great for everyday heroes looking for a bite on the go.

PREP TIME
10 minutes

COOKING TIME
20 minutes

YIELD
1 serving

DIFFICULTY
Easy

FOR THE ONIONS

1 tablespoon unsalted butter

1 cup sliced onions

½ teaspoon kosher salt

¼ teaspoon black pepper

FOR THE SANDWICH

4 ounces pastrami

1 tablespoon unsalted butter, softened

2 slices rye bread

2 slices Swiss cheese

1 tablespoon yellow mustard

5 pickle slices

TO MAKE THE ONIONS:

In a medium skillet over medium-high heat, add the butter and onions. Cook for 15 minutes until browned. Season with salt and pepper. Remove from pan and set aside.

TO MAKE THE SANDWICH:

Wipe out the same skillet. Over medium heat, add the pastrami and cook for 2 to 3 minutes, until warmed through. Remove from the pan and set aside.

Wipe out the skillet again. Butter one side of each slice of bread, place into the skillet buttered side down, over medium heat. Add a slice of cheese onto each piece of bread. Cook for 2 minutes, until the cheese has melted.

Add the mustard to one of the slices of bread, then top with the pastrami, onions, cheese, and pickles. Add the mustard to the other slices of bread. Flip the second slice of bread, with the mustard side down, onto the pickles. Use a spatula to press the sandwich down, making it extra flat.

Remove from pan, slice in half, and serve.

"WITH PICKLES. AND CAN YOU SMUSH IT DOWN REAL FLAT?"

– PETER PARKER

SPIDER-MAN: HOMECOMING

LARBY LARB

Peter's aunt, May, has seen her fair share of culinary disasters. After she burns their turkey meatloaf, May and Peter make their way to a local Thai restaurant. A fun twist on the Parkers' go-to meal, Larby Larb presents flavorful pork inside delicate lettuce cups to create a fresh, invigorating dish that's certain to have diners declaring, "I larb you."

GF

PREP TIME
15 minutes

COOKING TIME
5 minutes

YIELD
4 servings

DIFFICULTY
Moderate

INGREDIENTS

2 tablespoons uncooked short grain rice

1 tablespoon vegetable oil

1 pound ground pork

2 large shallots, peeled and sliced

2 Thai chiles, thinly sliced

2 tablespoons lime juice

1 tablespoon fish sauce

½ cup cilantro, chopped

½ cup fresh mint leaves, chopped

Bibb lettuce leaves, for serving

1 cucumber, sliced, for serving

Cooked white rice, for serving

In a dry skillet over medium heat, toast the rice grains for 8 to 10 minutes, until golden brown. Let cool slightly, then use a spice grinder to grind the toasted rice into a powder. Set aside.

In the same skillet over medium-high heat, add the oil and cook the ground pork for 5 to 6 minutes, until no longer pink.

Stir in the rice powder, shallots, chiles, lime juice, and fish sauce. Cook for 1 minute more.

Stir in the cilantro and mint leaves. Serve in the lettuce leaves, along with the cucumbers and rice.

"WHAT'S THE MATTER? I THOUGHT YOU LOVED LARB. IS IT TOO LARBY? NOT LARBY ENOUGH?"

– MAY PARKER

SPIDER-MAN: HOMECOMING

SPIDEY CHURRO BITES

In an effort to prove his worth as a friendly neighborhood Spider-Man, Peter Parker calls Happy Hogan to inform him that he stopped a bicycle theft and helped an old lady. The latter was grateful enough to reward Peter's altruism with a churro. In a sweet nod to both the kindness of strangers and Spidey's colorful suit, this homemade churro recipe blends cinnamon with red and blue sanding sugar. Crunchy, bold, and decidedly daring, churros are the perfect treat to serve to friends, family, or anyone who's offered a bit of extra help—Super Hero or otherwise!

V

PREP TIME
15 minutes

COOKING TIME
15 minutes

YIELD
24 churros

DIFFICULTY
Moderate

INGREDIENTS

1 cup water
2 tablespoons granulated sugar
2 tablespoons unsalted butter
1 teaspoon vanilla extract
¼ teaspoon kosher salt
1 cup all-purpose flour, sifted
1 large egg, beaten
1 teaspoon cinnamon
¼ teaspoon nutmeg
4 cups vegetable oil, for frying
¼ cup red sanding sugar
¼ cup blue sanding sugar

In a medium saucepan over medium-high heat, add the water, sugar, butter, vanilla, and salt. Bring to a boil.

Rapidly stir in the flour until just combined.

Remove from heat. Stir in the egg, cinnamon, and nutmeg until smooth.

Spoon the dough into a pastry bag fitted with a star-shaped tip.

Add the oil to a large Dutch oven. Bring the temperature to 350°F.

Pipe 4-inch strips of dough directly into the hot oil. Cook for 1 to 2 minutes per side until golden brown. Let drain on a wire rack.

Immediately sprinkle with the red and blue sanding sugars to serve.

"I HELPED THIS LOST, OLD DOMINICAN LADY. SHE WAS REALLY NICE AND BOUGHT ME A CHURRO."

– PETER PARKER

THOR: RAGNAROK

GRANDMASTER'S MELTY GRILLED CHEESE

V

PREP TIME
10 minutes

COOKING TIME
10 minutes

YIELD
1 serving

DIFFICULTY
Easy

The Grandmaster of Sakaar is about as eccentric—and deadly—as they come. Those who cross him tremble at the sight of the melt stick, a rod that reduces the Grandmaster's victims to a brilliant blue goo. But should the Grandmaster so desire, the melt stick could be put to much better use. Grandmaster's Melty Grilled Cheese represents one such purpose, melting a generous portion of shredded, blue-tinted cheese, which is placed between thick slices of crusty brioche bread. This classic comfort food would be sure to please even the mercurial Grandmaster himself.

INGREDIENTS

¼ cup shredded mozzarella cheese

¼ cup shredded pepper jack cheese

¼ teaspoon blue food coloring

2 slices brioche

2 tablespoons unsalted butter, softened, divided

1 tablespoon grated Parmesan cheese, divided

In a bowl, stir together the mozzarella cheese and pepper jack cheese with the blue food coloring, until dyed. Set aside.

Spread half the butter onto one side of a slice of bread. Sprinkle with half the Parmesan cheese. Place buttered side down into the skillet.

Top with dyed cheeses.

Place the second slice of bread on top. Spread the remaining butter onto the top of the bread and sprinkle with the remaining Parmesan cheese.

Turn the heat to medium. Cook for 2 to 3 minutes each side until golden brown and the cheese has melted. Slice to serve.

Marvel Studios' *Thor: Ragnarok* (2017)

THOR: RAGNAROK

VALKYRIE'S PEGASUS PUNCH

GF, V, V+

PREP TIME
10 minutes

FREEZING TIME
Overnight

YIELD
1 serving

DIFFICULTY
Easy

Valkyrie once belonged to a fierce squadron of shieldmaidens sworn to defend the Asgardian throne. Atop their winged horses, these warriors flew into battle against Hela, the Goddess of Death, and, despite their fighting prowess, only Valkyrie survived the encounter. She exiled herself to Sakaar, where she is known as Scrapper 142 and spends her time sampling the planet's various libations. This punch invokes the brilliant colors of Valkyrie's adopted planet. Green, blue, red, and orange ice cubes are doused in lemon-lime soda, creating a vibrant color palette worthy of Sakaar's jubilant culture.

INGREDIENTS

¼ cup blue sports drink
¼ cup fruit punch
¼ cup green sports drink
¼ cup orange juice
2 sprigs fresh mint, divided
1 cup lemon lime soda
1 orange slice, for garnish

Into an ice cube tray pour the blue sports drink, fruit punch, green sports drink, and orange juice into separate mold sections. Freeze overnight.

Muddle one sprig of mint in the bottom of a glass.

Unmold the ice cubes and add to the glass.

Pour the lemon lime soda over the ice cubes.

Garnish with the orange slice and remaining mint to serve.

Marvel Studios' *Thor: Ragnarok* (2017)

THOR: RAGNAROK

THE CUPCAKE OF CHAMPIONS

V

PREP TIME
1 hour

COOKING TIME
20 minutes

YIELD
18 cupcakes

DIFFICULTY
Moderate

Upon being captured by Valkyrie and made to fight in the Contest of Champions, Thor is thrilled to discover that his opponent isn't the undefeatable killing machine suggested by the Grandmaster. Rather, the Hulk offers a *very* familiar face. Such news is certainly worthy of a celebration, and there's no finer way to celebrate a happy reunion than by sharing a platter of cupcakes. This colorful recipe blends sugar, flour, and cocoa into delightfully sweet cakes that are topped with green icing and decorated to look like the Grandmaster's favorite champion. This dessert is perfect for sharing with just about anyone—including friends from work!

FOR THE CUPCAKES

2 cups all-purpose flour
⅓ cup cocoa powder
½ teaspoon baking powder
½ teaspoon baking soda
½ teaspoon kosher salt
½ cup unsalted butter
1 cup granulated sugar
½ cup light brown sugar
2 large eggs
½ teaspoon vanilla extract
1 cup buttermilk

FOR THE FROSTING

1 cup unsalted butter, softened
4 cups confectioners' sugar
1 teaspoon vanilla extract
4 to 6 tablespoons whole milk, as needed
1 tablespoon green food coloring

FOR THE DECORATION

4.4 ounces black fondant
4.4 ounces white fondant

TO MAKE THE CUPCAKES:

Preheat the oven to 350°F. Prep a cupcake pan with liners.

In a medium bowl, whisk together the flour, cocoa powder, baking powder, baking soda, and salt. Set aside.

In the bowl of an electric mixer, cream the butter, sugar, and brown sugar. Add the eggs and vanilla until just combined.

Alternate adding the flour mixture and the buttermilk to the bowl of the electric mixer until combined.

Fill the liners two-thirds full and bake for 17 to 19 minutes depending on your oven. Let cool on a wire rack.

TO MAKE THE FROSTING:

In the bowl of an electric mixer, cream the butter while adding the confectioners' sugar a little at a time.

Add the vanilla, milk, and green food coloring. Turn the mixer up to medium high and whip for 10 to 15 seconds until fluffy.

Prep a baking sheet with parchment. Pipe the frosting onto the cupcakes. Flip upside down onto the parchment, to flatten the frosting. Refrigerate for 30 minutes until firm.

TO DECORATE THE CUPCAKES:

Peel off of the parchment. On the flattened frosting, use the black and white fondant to create Hulk faces on the cupcakes.

BLACK PANTHER

HEART-SHAPED HERB LEMONADE

According to Wakandan lore, the Panther Goddess Bast guided a warrior shaman to the Heart-Shaped Herb—an indigo plant that, when ingested, grants superhuman speed, strength, and prowess. The warrior consumed the herb and became the first in a long line of Black Panthers, whose strength and honor unite the tribes of Wakanda. Like those before him, T'Challa drank the herb and was imbued with the powers of the Black Panther—and its responsibilities. Heart-Shaped Herb Lemonade is a sweet, purple-hued concoction that draws inspiration from Wakanda's mystical plant. Made with dried hibiscus, turmeric, and ginger and packed with healthy antioxidants, this lemonade might not come with a crown . . . but it's sure to give you the strength you'll need to get through the day. Wakanda forever!

GF, V

PREP TIME
5 minutes

COOKING TIME
5 minutes

YIELD
4 servings

DIFFICULTY
Easy

INGREDIENTS

8 cups water, plus more for rinsing

1 cup dried hibiscus

One 2-inch knob fresh turmeric

One 2-inch knob fresh ginger

½ teaspoon dried whole cloves

½ cup freshly squeezed lemon juice

Honey

Ice

Add water to a medium-sized pot and bring to a boil. Reduce the heat to low after it begins to boil.

Rinse the hibiscus with cold water and drain it well.

Add the hibiscus, turmeric, ginger, and cloves to the hot water, and leave on low heat to cook for 5 minutes.

Remove the pot from heat and steep until water cools to room temperature.

Strain the liquid into a pitcher then stir in the lemon juice and honey to taste until dissolved.

Serve over ice. Store in an airtight pitcher or jar in the fridge for up to two weeks.

"HE OR SHE WHO CONSUMES THE HEART-SHAPED HERB BECOMES THE BLACK PANTHER."

– SHURI

BLACK PANTHER

SHURI'S BHAJIAS

Wakandan princess Shuri's masterful command of technology ensures that both the Black Panther and the Dora Milaje are equipped with cutting-edge armor and weaponry. But leading the Wakandan Design Group while simultaneously fulfilling her royal duties can be consuming work. And these flavorful bhajias would make the perfect snack for long hours spent in the lab. Here, homemade potato fritters are dusted with ginger, cumin, and cilantro, seasoned with hot sauce and fried to perfection. Sure to be the hit of any late-night work session, Shuri's Bhajias pack a spicy punch—just like the warrior scientist who inspires them.

V, V+

PREP TIME
10 minutes

COOKING TIME
5 minutes

YIELD
4 servings

DIFFICULTY
Difficult

INGREDIENTS

½ cup gram flour
1 tablespoon corn flour
1 teaspoon minced ginger
2 teaspoons ground cumin
1 teaspoon hot sauce of choice
½ teaspoon salt
½ cup finely chopped fresh cilantro
⅓ cup water
2 large russet potatoes
Vegetable oil, for frying

In a large bowl, combine the gram flour, corn flour, ginger, cumin, hot sauce, salt, and cilantro.

Add the water to the flour mixture gradually. A paste should form, thick enough to coat the back of a spoon.

Using a sharp knife or mandoline, thinly slice the potatoes crosswise.

Add the potatoes to the flour mixture, making sure each slice is coated evenly.

Line a large baking sheet with paper towels. Heat some oil in a large skillet over high heat. Fry the potatoes in the oil for 3 to 4 minutes, until they turn golden brown.

Remove the bhajias from the oil with a slotted spoon and transfer them to the prepped baking sheet.

Serve immediately.

Marvel Studios' *Black Panther* (2018)

RIVER TRIBE TILAPIA WITH EFO RIRO

PREP TIME	COOKING TIME	YIELD	DIFFICULTY
10 minutes	30 minutes	4 servings	Easy

When a vibrainum-rich meteorite crashed into Earth, several tribes battled for control of the precious resource before eventually uniting as the Kingdom of Wakanda. Although the Jabari Tribe remains isolated in the mountains, the Mining Tribe, the Merchant Tribe, the Border Tribe, and the River Tribe each play unique roles within the kingdom—with the latter tending to the waters that run through the region. River Tribe Tilapia with Efo Riro offers a spicy nod to the water-faring tribe. It pairs suya-coated tilapia with a verdant Nigerian spinach stew, creating a crowd-pleasing dish that's sure to bring people together—no coronation challenge required.

FOR THE TILAPIA

½ cup all-purpose flour

1 tablespoon suya spice

1 teaspoon garlic powder

1 teaspoon onion powder

1 teaspoon chili powder

½ teaspoon ground cumin

Four 6-ounce tilapia filets

Kosher salt

Freshly ground black pepper

2 tablespoons vegetable oil

FOR THE EFO RIRO

3 large red bell peppers

1 scotch bonnet pepper (or 1 jalapeño, if you prefer a milder dish)

1 medium onion, sliced

¼ cup palm oil

2 tablespoons dried crayfish powder

1 vegetable bouillon cube

Salt

½ cup water

1½ pounds spinach, blanched

TO MAKE THE TILAPIA:

In a large bowl, whisk to combine together the flour, suya spice, garlic powder, onion powder, chili powder, and cumin.

Season the tilapia filets generously with salt and pepper to taste, then dip each fillet into the seasoned flour, shaking off any excess flour. Place on a clean plate or baking sheet.

Heat a large, nonstick skillet over medium heat. Add the vegetable oil. Add the fillets, 2 at a time, and cook 3 to 4 minutes per side, until the crust is golden brown.

TO MAKE THE EFO RIRO:

Puree the bell peppers, scotch bonnet peppers, and half the onion in a blender. Warning: Scotch bonnets are very hot, so remove the seeds and pith for a slightly milder taste.

Heat the palm oil in a large skillet over medium to high heat. Add the remaining sliced onion and fry until golden brown, about 5 minutes.

Add the blended bell pepper sauce and fry until the sauce begins to thicken up, about 15 minutes. Stir consistently to prevent the sauce from burning.

Add in the crayfish powder, bouillon cube, and salt to taste. Stir until everything is well combined.

Add ½ cup water, stir together, and allow to simmer for 5 minutes.

Add the spinach and mix well. Cover and allow to cook 5 minutes, stirring every so often.

Serve the tilapia over the efo riro.

WEST AFRICAN FRIED CHICKEN AND PLANTAIN WAFFLES

PREP TIME
45 minutes, plus an additional 1 hour for marinating and 8 to 12 hours for dissolving

COOKING TIME
40 minutes

YIELD
4 servings

DIFFICULTY
Moderate

Growing up in Oakland, California, Erik Killmonger—son of Wakanda's Prince N'Jobu—knew what it was like to live between two worlds. His feet were firmly planted in California, while his heart dreamed of seeing a Wakandan sunset—a sight his father told him was the most beautiful in the world. Inspired by Erik's upbringing, this fusion recipe combines a classic American staple with a delectable West African side. Crispy buttermilk fried chicken is seasoned with suya spice, smoked paprika, and a hearty dash of hot sauce, while plantain waffles are sweetened with vanilla and coconut oil, then doused in mango syrup. Sweet, savory, and decidedly delicious, West African Fried Chicken and Plantain Waffles could be right at home anywhere—just like Erik Killmonger himself.

FOR THE BRINE

2 cups buttermilk
1 tablespoon kosher salt
½ tablespoon garlic powder
½ tablespoon onion powder
1 tablespoon suya spice
1 tablespoon hot sauce of your choice
1 teaspoon smoked paprika

FOR THE FRIED CHICKEN

8 boneless, skinless chicken thighs
Peanut oil, for deep frying
3 cups all-purpose flour
⅓ cup cornstarch
2 teaspoons baking powder
2 teaspoons onion powder
2 teaspoons kosher salt
1 tablespoon suya spice
2 teaspoons black pepper

TO MAKE THE BRINE:

Whisk the buttermilk, salt, garlic powder, onion powder, suya spice, hot sauce, and smoked paprika together in a large mixing bowl.

Add the chicken thighs to the bowl, making sure every thigh is covered in the buttermilk brine. Cover the bowl with plastic wrap and let the chicken marinate in the brine for at least 1 hour. Chicken can be left to marinate overnight in the refrigerator.

TO MAKE THE FRIED CHICKEN:

In a large pot, add half a pot's worth of oil. Heat it to 350°F.

While the oil is heating up, in a mixing bowl whisk together flour, cornstarch, baking powder, onion powder, salt, suya spice, and black pepper. Take each chicken thigh from the brine and dredge into the seasoned flour. Thoroughly coat the chicken with the seasoned flour, then let rest on a rack for five minutes before frying.

Fry the chicken thighs in the hot oil (no more than about 4 thighs per batch) for 8 to 9 minutes until golden brown, crispy, and cooked through completely.

Carefully take the chicken thighs out of the oil and place them on a baking sheet fitted with a wire rack and let cool slightly before serving. Repeat until all the chicken thighs are fried.

FOR THE PLANTAIN WAFFLES

1 cup sliced ripe plantain

¼ cup cassava flour

⅛ teaspoon salt

½ teaspoon cinnamon

½ teaspoon vanilla extract (optional)

1 tablespoon coconut oil

FOR THE MANGO SYRUP

The pits and peels of 4 large mangoes

1 lemon rind

1 cup brown sugar

TO MAKE THE PLANTAIN WAFFLES:

Add the plantains to a blender. Blend for a few seconds, stop to scrape the sides, then blend for a few more seconds until the plantains are mostly smooth.

Add the cassava flour, salt, cinnamon, vanilla extract (if using), and coconut oil to the blender. Blend until batter is smooth, stopping to scrape the sides every so often.

Scoop ¼ cup batter onto preheated mini waffle iron and cook per the manufacturer's instructions. Set aside for serving.

TO MAKE THE MANGO SYRUP:

Combine the mango pits and peels with the lemon rind and brown sugar in a large mixing bowl. Toss to combine, then cover the bowl tightly with plastic wrap and let stand at room temperature overnight until sugar has completely dissolved, between 8 to 12 hours.

Transfer to a strainer over a glass bowl, pressing the peels and pits gently with a spatula to extract out the syrup. Refrigerate and store syrup in a glass jar for up to 2 weeks.

Serve the fried chicken on top of the plantain waffles, then drizzle generously with the mango syrup.

BLACK PANTHER

THE DORA MILAJE'S PILAU

The Dora Milaje are an elite squad of female warriors tasked with protecting the ruler of Wakanda. Trained in martial arts, these royal bodyguards carry vibranium spears and communicate using Kimoyo beads. Such a role requires both vigilance and vigor, and no doubt requires a steady supply of protein-packed meals. Loaded with vegetables, spice, and a liberal amount of cubed beef, The Dora Milaje's Pilau is a fragrant rice dish that would be perfectly paired with a hard day of training—no matter the location. After all, the Dora Milaje have jurisdiction wherever the Dora Milaje find themselves to be.

GF

PREP TIME
10 minutes

COOKING TIME
40 minutes

YIELD
6 servings

DIFFICULTY
Moderate

INGREDIENTS

¼ cup vegetable oil

2 medium red onions, thinly sliced

4 garlic cloves, minced

2 tablespoons minced ginger

1 serrano chile, finely chopped

1 pound beef sirloin, cubed into bite-sized pieces

1 tablespoon pilau masala

2 beef bouillon cubes

2 bay leaves

¼ cup roughly chopped fresh cilantro

Salt

3 Roma tomatoes, diced

5 medium Yukon gold potatoes, peeled and cut into quarters

4 cups water

2 cups basmati rice

Heat a large pot over medium-high heat. Add the oil.

Add the sliced onions and fry for 10 minutes or until the onion starts to turn golden brown.

Add the garlic, ginger, and serrano chile. Cook for 1 to 2 minutes, until fragrant.

Add the cubed beef, pilau masala, beef bouillon cubes, bay leaves, cilantro, and salt to taste. Cook until the meat browns and caramelizes, stirring occasionally for 8 to 10 minutes.

Add the diced tomatoes and cook for 5 minutes until the tomatoes have released their liquid.

Stir in the potatoes. Add the water and bring to a boil. Simmer for 10 minutes.

Stir in the rice. Cover the pot with a piece of aluminum foil, then with the pot lid. Reduce the heat to low and cook for 20 minutes until the rice is cooked and the liquid is absorbed.

Fluff the rice with a fork and serve immediately.

Marvel Studios'
Black Panther (2018)

BORDER TRIBE LEMON CHICKEN

Tasked with protecting Wakanda's borders, members of the Border Tribe maintain the region's cloaking devices. Like its namesake tribe, this no-nonsense chicken dish may appear unassuming—but one bite will have dinner guests clamoring for another invitation. Prepared with mustard and habañero chile and marinated with lemon and onion, Border Tribe Lemon Chicken is a comforting West African dish that's sure to draw a curious crowd!

GF

PREP TIME
10 minutes, plus 3 hours to marinate

COOKING TIME
1 hour, 10 minutes

YIELD
4 servings

DIFFICULTY
Easy

INGREDIENTS

4 boneless, skinless chicken thighs

4 chicken drumsticks

4 cups sliced onions

⅓ cup fresh lemon juice

1 teaspoon salt

½ teaspoon black pepper

1 small habañero chile, seeded and minced

1½ tablespoons peanut oil

1½ cups chicken stock

½ cup pimento-stuffed olives

½ cup water

1 tablespoon Dijon mustard

Rice, for serving

Place the chicken thighs and drumsticks in a large resealable bag.

Add the onions, lemon juice, salt, black pepper, and habañero chile to the bag. Seal the bag and massage the chicken with the contents of the bag. Place the bag in the refrigerator for 3 hours to marinate.

Heat the oil in a large Dutch oven over medium-high heat. Add all the contents of the bag to the Dutch oven. Cook for 10 minutes, browning the chicken. Add the stock, olives, water, and Dijon mustard.

Bring the mixture to a boil, then reduce the heat to medium-low and simmer, uncovered, for 1 hour.

Serve over rice.

Marvel Studios' *Black Panther* (2018)

BLACK PANTHER

JABARI TRIBE PEANUT STEW

GF, V, V+

PREP TIME
10 minutes

COOKING TIME
30 minutes

YIELD
6 servings

DIFFICULTY
Easy

The leader of the Jabari Tribe makes for an intimidating presence. With his muscular stature and unyielding expression, the warrior ruler is the picture of power. But M'Baku has a few surprises up his fur-cloaked sleeve—from his cheeky sense of humor to his dietary preferences. Jabari Tribe Peanut Stew is a dish the isolated clan's noble leader might have shared with his family. Tomatoes, onions, potatoes, and carrots are seasoned with spices and cooked with creamy peanut butter. Simmered in a savory broth and served with a hearty helping of rice, this delightful stew is bound to win diners over. "*Mayafa*!"

INGREDIENTS

¼ cup vegetable oil
2 medium tomatoes, roughly chopped
1 medium onion, roughly chopped, divided
3 to 4 cloves garlic
3 tablespoons dried parsley
1 teaspoon smoked paprika
1 tablespoon cayenne pepper
½ teaspoon white pepper
3 cups vegetable stock
¾ pound russet potatoes, roughly chopped
¼ pound carrots, roughly chopped
½ cup smooth peanut butter
1 small habanero chile, diced
3 cups vegetable stock
Salt
Black pepper
Cooked white rice, for serving

Heat the vegetable oil in a large pot over medium heat.

Combine the tomatoes, half of the chopped onion, garlic, and parsley in a blender. Blend the ingredients until they are completely smooth.

Add the remaining half of the chopped onion to the pot and cook for 2 minutes. Pour the blended tomato mixture into the pot. Add the smoked paprika, cayenne, and white pepper. Stir to combine.

Cook for 10 minutes. Add the potatoes, carrots, peanut butter, habañero, and vegetable stock.

Stir the ingredients together and continue to cook for 10 to 15 minutes, until the potatoes are tender.

Season with salt and black pepper to taste..

Serve with rice.

> "IF YOU SAY ONE MORE WORD, I'LL FEED YOU TO MY CHILDREN! I'M KIDDING, WE'RE VEGETARIANS."
>
> – M'BAKU

AVENGERS: INFINITY WAR

STARK RAVING HAZELNUTS

Some promises are made to be broken. Tony Stark's vow to avoid dairy ended with the arrival of Stark Raving Hazelnuts, an ice cream flavor named after the enigmatic Avenger. However, this vegan variation would have allowed him to keep his word while still partaking in his namesake dessert. This version of Stark Raving Hazelnuts takes a coffee ice cream base and mixes in toasted hazelnuts with chocolate chunks. Sweet, savory, and imbued with the power to bring people together—just like the Avengers themselves—this dessert is the ideal, icy treat to mark the end of a long day or the beginning of an intergalactic battle.

GF, V, V+

PREP TIME
15 minutes

FREEZING TIME
8 hours

COOKING TIME
10 minutes

YIELD
6 servings

DIFFICULTY
Easy

INGREDIENTS

½ cup hazelnuts

Two 15-ounce cans coconut cream, chilled overnight

½ cup confectioners' sugar

1 tablespoon espresso powder

1 tablespoon vanilla extract

¼ teaspoon kosher salt

½ cup chopped dark chocolate

Preheat the oven to 300°F. Place the hazelnuts on a parchment-lined baking sheet. Bake for 10 minutes. Transfer the nuts to a clean kitchen towel. Let cool. Rub with the towel to remove the skins. Chop roughly and set aside.

Carefully open the chilled cans of coconut cream. Scoop out the cream, and place it into a large chilled mixing bowl. Discard or keep the coconut water for another recipe. With a handheld electric mixer, whip the coconut cream until creamy.

Stir in the confectioners' sugar, espresso powder, vanilla, and salt. Set aside.

Pour half of the ice cream mixture into a chilled loaf pan. Sprinkle in half the diced hazelnuts, and stir to swirl. Top with the remaining coconut cream mixture, then the remaining hazelnuts and chopped chocolate. Use a knife to swirl the mixture.

Cover with plastic wrap. Freeze for 8 hours or overnight.

Scoop to serve.

Marvel Studios' *Avengers: Infinity War* (2018)

AVENGERS: INFINITY WAR

WONG'S FAVORITE HULK-INSPIRED FUDGE ICE CREAM

After many years spent off-world, Bruce Banner is shocked to discover that the people of Earth have named an ice cream after him. In a nod to the fiery temper of "the other guy," Hulk's namesake flavor combines a touch of cayenne pepper with cinnamon-chocolate ice cream and chunks of fudge brownie. Rich and chocolaty, it's sure to be a smash hit.

V

PREP TIME
15 minutes

FREEZING TIME
8 hours

YIELD
6 servings

DIFFICULTY
Easy

INGREDIENTS

6 ounces dark chocolate

One 14-ounce can sweetened condensed milk

1 teaspoon vanilla extract

1 teaspoon cinnamon

¼ teaspoon cayenne pepper

¼ teaspoon kosher salt

2 cups heavy cream

1 cup diced fudge brownies

2 tablespoons mini chocolate chips

In a double boiler over low heat, melt the dark chocolate. Set aside to cool.

In a large bowl, combine the cooled chocolate, sweetened condensed milk, vanilla, cinnamon, cayenne pepper, and salt. Set aside.

In a separate large, chilled bowl, whip the heavy cream with an electric mixer until stiff peaks form. Fold into the chocolate mixture.

Pour half of the ice cream mixture into a chilled loaf pan. Sprinkle half the brownies and stir to swirl. Top with the remaining ice cream mixture, then the remaining brownies and the chocolate chips. Use a knife to swirl the mixture.

Cover with plastic wrap. Freeze for 8 hours or overnight.

Scoop to serve.

Marvel Studios' *Avengers: Infinity War* (2018)

AVENGERS: INFINITY WAR

WONG'S TUNA MELT

As a highly trained sorcerer, Wong understands that "attachment to the material is detachment from the spiritual." As a result, he rarely carries money—a practice that complicates his life outside of Kamar-Taj. But for the times when he's craving a non-metaphysical meal, this tuna melt would be sure to hit the spot. Made from salty tuna, melted cheese, and two slices of toasted sourdough, Wong's Tuna Melt is a tasty nod to his preferred deli order—no sorcery required.

PREP TIME
10 minutes

COOKING TIME
10 minutes

YIELD
1 serving

DIFFICULTY
Easy

INGREDIENTS

One 5-ounce can tuna in water, drained

3 tablespoons mayonnaise

1 tablespoon diced celery

1 tablespoon diced cornichons

1 tablespoon diced red onion

1 teaspoon yellow mustard

¼ teaspoon kosher salt

⅛ teaspoon lemon pepper

Dash hot sauce

2 slices sourdough bread

2 tablespoons unsalted butter, softened

2 slices tomato

2 slices cheddar cheese

In a medium bowl, stir the tuna, mayonnaise, celery, cornichons, red onion, mustard, salt, lemon pepper, and hot sauce, until just combined.

Butter one side of each slice of bread.

Onto a plate, place one slice buttered side down, then spoon on the tuna mixture. Top with cheese and tomato slices.

Place the other slice of bread buttered side up, on top of the tomato slices.

In a skillet over medium heat, place the sandwich into the pan. Cook for 2 to 3 minutes, until browned. Flip and cook for 2 to 3 minutes more, until browned.

"I WOULDN'T SAY NO TO A TUNA MELT."

– WONG

AVENGERS: INFINITY WAR

THE SOUL SCONE

In his quest for power, Thanos procures the Soul Stone, after making a heartbreaking sacrifice on Vormir. Luckily, the orange-hued Soul Scone requires no such sacrifice. In fact, it's all but certain to bring people together! With citrusy undertones and a burst of flavorful mango, this refreshingly sweet pastry is so good that it's sure to be gone in a snap.

V

PREP TIME
10 minutes

COOKING TIME
15 minutes

YIELD
24 scones

DIFFICULTY
Easy

INGREDIENTS

½ cup granulated sugar

1 tablespoon orange zest

2½ cups all-purpose flour

1 tablespoon baking powder

½ teaspoon ground ginger

¼ teaspoon kosher salt

½ cup (1 stick) unsalted butter, melted

1 large egg, beaten

1 cup buttermilk

1 teaspoon clear vanilla extract

¾ cup diced dried mango

¼ cup heavy cream, for brushing

2 tablespoons coarse sanding sugar

Preheat the oven to 400°F. Prep baking sheets with parchment.

In a small bowl, stir together the sugar and orange zest. Set aside.

In a large bowl whisk together the flour, baking powder, ginger, and salt. Stir in the orange sugar.

Make a well in the center of the dry ingredients and stir in the butter, egg, buttermilk, and vanilla until just combined. Fold in the dried mango. Refrigerate dough for 15 minutes.

Use a 2-tablespoon scoop to form rounds. Place 2 inches apart onto the prepped baking sheets.

Brush with heavy cream. Sprinkle with sanding sugar.

Bake for 15 minutes. Transfer to a wire rack to cool.

Marvel Studios' *Avengers: Infinity War* (2018)

AVENGERS: INFINITY WAR

INFINITEA

If you've baked all six Infinity Scones, unite them with an out-of-this-world Infinitea! Gather your scones, make a pitcher of this refreshing pineapple and peach tea, and now you're 14,000,605 times closer to becoming the most powerful tea party host in the univers

GF, V, V+

PREP TIME
15 minutes

COOKING TIME
15 minutes

YIELD
10 servings

DIFFICULTY
Moderate

FOR THE PEACH PUREE

2 cups sliced peaches

1 cup water

¾ cup granulated sugar

2 ginger slices

FOR THE TEA

4 green tea bags

6 cups boiling water

1 cup crushed pineapple, for garnish

2 peaches, sliced, for garnish

TO MAKE THE PEACH PUREE:

In a saucepan over medium-high heat, add the peaches, water, sugar, and ginger. Bring to a boil. Turn the heat down to low and simmer for 15 minutes, until fragrant. Remove the ginger and let cool.

Pour mixture into the jar of a blender. Blend until smooth. Pour through a sieve to remove clumps. Place in a sealable container and refrigerate until ready to use.

TO MAKE THE TEA:

In a large container, add the tea bags and boiling water. Let steep for 4 minutes. Remove tea bags and refrigerate the tea until cold.

In a large pitcher, combine the peach puree and brewed tea and stir to mix well.

Add ice to tall glasses. Pour the tea over the ice, top each glass with a spoonful of crushed pineapple and a peach slice, and serve.

Marvel Studios' *Avengers: Infinity War* (2018)

X-CON FANCY PASTRIES

Scott Lang and his former prison mate Luis, along with ex-con associates Kurt and Dave, establish X-Con Security Consultants, a company that provides home safety systems throughout the San Francisco Bay Area. But since their budget is tight—and in fact, X-Con is often just days away from shutting down—the group can only afford to put out their best snacks when an important client drops by. These fancy pastries honor the company's humble beginnings. Bake them in advance, then bring them out any time company swings by. As the X-Cons would say, "We got you covered!"

V

PREP TIME
15 minutes

COOKING TIME
30 minutes

YIELD
6 servings

DIFFICULTY
Moderate

INGREDIENTS

One 8.5-ounce sheet puff pastry, thawed

½ cup cream cheese

1 tablespoon confectioners' sugar

1 teaspoon lemon zest

½ teaspoon vanilla extract

⅓ cup raspberry jam

1 large egg beaten with 1 tablespoon water, for egg wash

2 tablespoons coarse sanding sugar

Preheat the oven to 375°F. Line a baking sheet with parchment.

Place the puff pastry onto the parchment. Set aside.

In a small bowl, stir together the cream cheese, confectioners' sugar, lemon zest, and vanilla. Spread the mixture into the middle third of the puff pastry, leaving a ½-inch border at the top and bottom. Spread the raspberry jam on top.

With a knife, cut the 2 outer areas into eight 1-inch-thick diagonal strips, stopping at the filling. Fold the ½-inch dough at the top over onto the filling.

Start folding the side pastry strips over the filling, alternating each side to create a braid.

Brush with the egg wash and sprinkle with the sanding sugar. Bake for 25 to 30 minutes until golden brown.

Allow to cool slightly. Cut into six pieces before serving.

"HEY, WHAT'S UP WITH THE FANCY PASTRIES? WE GOTTA KEEP THE FOOD BUDGET DOWN!"

– LUIS

ANT-MAN AND THE WASP

JIMMY WOO'S MAGIC NOODLES

PREP TIME
10 minutes

COOKING TIME
45 minutes

YIELD
8 servings

DIFFICULTY
Moderate

FBI Agent Jimmy Woo has big dreams. Beyond chasing down bad guys, he hopes to one day master some simple magic tricks—a feat that has so far proven to be elusive. But crafting these amazing, floating noodles is surprisingly simple, and it's sure to impress a crowd! With nothing more than an apple, two sticks, and some artfully arranged pasta, even a struggling magician can execute an illusion rivaling anything that the Reality Stone can conjure up.

INGREDIENTS

2 tablespoons olive oil
1 medium onion, diced
2 garlic cloves, minced
1 pound ground beef
One 28-ounce can crushed tomatoes
One 15-ounce can tomato sauce
1 tablespoon tomato paste
1 tablespoon dried basil
1 tablespoon dried oregano
1 tablespoon dried parsley
1 teaspoon onion powder
1 teaspoon paprika
1 teaspoon kosher salt
½ teaspoon black pepper
One 16-ounce package spaghetti
1 apple, halved
½ cup grated Parmesan cheese, for serving
¼ cup chopped fresh parsley, for serving

In a Dutch oven over medium-high heat, add the olive oil and cook the onion and garlic for 3 to 4 minutes, until softened.

Add the ground beef and cook for 7 to 8 minutes until browned.

Stir in the crushed tomatoes, tomato sauce, tomato paste, basil, oregano, parsley, onion powder, paprika, salt, and pepper. Turn heat to low. Cover and simmer for 30 minutes.

Cook spaghetti according to package directions. Drain but do not rinse.

Toss the spaghetti with the sauce. Set aside.

To serve, place the apple flat side down into a serving dish. Cover with a spoonful of spaghetti.

Wedge two skewers into the tines of a fork. Pierce into the apple to stand the fork up. Cover with more spaghetti to give the fork the illusion of floating.

Sprinkle with Parmesan cheese and fresh parsley to serve.

Marvel Studios' *Ant-Man and The Wasp* (2018)

ANT-MAN AND THE WASP

SAN FRANCISCO CLAM CHOWDER

PREP TIME
25 minutes

COOKING TIME
30 minutes

YIELD
6 servings

DIFFICULTY
Moderate

The City by the Bay is known for many things. It's home to Alcatraz, Ant-Man, and some of the best clam chowder in the world. This San Francisco Clam Chowder serves up a hearty portion of a food that Scott Lang might well have enjoyed—when he wasn't busy returning things he stole, of course. Chopped clams are boiled with clam juice, potatoes, and a bounty of spices, then mixed with a healthy dose of heavy cream and topped with bacon. It's a guaranteed crowd-pleaser that's bound to have dinner guests clam-oring for more . . . and saying "thanks for thinking of me!" Just like Ant-Man himself.

INGREDIENTS

6 bacon slices, diced
2 tablespoons unsalted butter
1 large onion, diced
2 celery ribs, diced
2 garlic cloves, minced
¼ cup all-purpose flour
½ teaspoon kosher salt
¼ teaspoon smoked paprika
¼ teaspoon white pepper
1 sprig fresh thyme
16 ounces clam juice
2 large russet potatoes, peeled and cubed
Three 6.5-ounce cans chopped clams, undrained
1 cup whole milk
1 cup heavy cream
1 tablespoon cornstarch dissolved in 2 tablespoons water, for slurry
Torn fresh parsley, for garnish

In a large Dutch oven over medium-high heat, add the bacon and cook for 10 minutes or until crispy. Let drain on a paper towel lined plate. Set aside.

Discard the bacon grease. Return the heat to medium, and add the butter, onions, celery, and garlic. Cook for 5 minutes, until softened.

Stir in the flour and cook for 2 to 3 minutes until slightly thickened.

Stir in the salt, paprika, white pepper, and thyme.

Add the clam juice, potatoes, and clams. Bring to a boil. Reduce to a simmer and cook for 10 to 15 minutes, until the potatoes are fork-tender.

Stir in the milk and heavy cream.

Stir in the cornstarch slurry and cooked bacon. Simmer on medium low for another 5 to 7 minutes.

Garnish with parsley to serve.

Marvel Studios' *Ant-Man and The Wasp* (2018)

TRUTH SERUM

X-Con Security Consultants are a ragtag group of former convicts who banded together to form a legitimate entrepreneurial enterprise. They're hardworking and loyal, and they would never, *ever* reveal one-another's secrets . . . until they're plied with a truth serum! When Luis is subjected to Uzman's concoction—one said to make anyone "suggestible and highly responsive"—he quickly discloses the history of Scott Lang's illicit activities . . . and unwittingly exposes his friend to a dangerous band of criminals. Made from strawberry syrup, club soda, and coconut cream, this recipe might not extract information from the unwilling, but it's sure to have anyone singing its praises—at a rapid pace!

GF, V, V+

PREP TIME
5 minutes

COOKING TIME
N/A

YIELD
1 serving

DIFFICULTY
Easy

INGREDIENTS

1 ½ ounces strawberry syrup
8 ounces club soda
3 tablespoons coconut cream
Mint, for garnish

Fill a tall glass with ice. Pour in the syrup, then the club soda. Gently stir.

Spoon the coconut cream over the top.

Add the mint to serve.

"OH, IS THAT TRUTH SERUM?"

– LUIS

"THERE'S NO SUCH THING AS TRUTH SERUM. THAT'S JUST NONSENSE FROM TV."

– UZMAN

CAPTAIN MARVEL

DIAGONALLY CUT FRENCH TOAST

On the trail of shape-shifting Skrulls, Carol Danvers demands that Nick Fury prove his identity by naming a detail so bizarre that a Skrull could never fabricate it. In doing so, she learns a savory piece of information about the S.H.I.E.L.D. agent—that he can't eat toast if it is cut diagonally. This French toast is crafted by dusting a fluffy brioche bun with maple and cinnamon, then cooking the concoction to perfection in a hot skillet. Sweet, rich, and cut into triangles, this recipe would have even the steadfast Nick Fury singing a different tune.

V

PREP TIME
10 minutes

COOKING TIME
5 minutes

YIELD
4 servings

DIFFICULTY
Easy

INGREDIENTS

4 large eggs

⅓ cup heavy cream

1 teaspoon vanilla extract

1 tablespoon maple syrup

1 teaspoon cinnamon

¼ teaspoon nutmeg

¼ teaspoon kosher salt

8 slices brioche

4 tablespoons unsalted butter

1 tablespoon confectioners' sugar, for dusting

In a shallow dish, whisk the eggs, heavy cream, vanilla, maple syrup, cinnamon, nutmeg, and salt.

Dip the brioche into the egg mixture.

In a large skillet over medium-high heat, melt the butter. Add the dipped bread pieces, cooking for 2 to 3 minutes on each side until golden brown.

Cut diagonally. Dust with confectioners' sugar to serve.

"IF TOAST IS CUT DIAGONALLY, I CAN'T EAT IT."

– NICK FURY

Marvel Studios' *Captain Marvel* (2019)

FLERKEN NIBBLES

When an unwitting Captain Marvel meets the famed Flerken, Goose, she's shocked to discover that the cat-like creature can seemingly consume *anything*—from a rubber duck to the Tesseract itself. Perhaps Goose wouldn't find herself quite so ravenous if her companions offered up a few of these filling Flerken Nibbles. Here, spinach and cheese are baked into flaky puff pastries. Topped with protrusions that are molded to resemble the Flerken's tentacles, these treats are an ideal snack for Skrull guests, S.H.I.E.L.D. agents, and everyone's favorite furball. (Publisher's note: Do not feed these to your cats, lest they scratch out your eye, like Goose did to Nick Fury.)

V

PREP TIME
15 minutes

COOKING TIME
20 minutes

YIELD
9 servings

DIFFICULTY
Moderate

INGREDIENTS

8 ounces frozen spinach, thawed

4 ounces cream cheese, softened

3 tablespoons feta cheese

2 garlic cloves, minced

¼ teaspoon kosher salt

¼ teaspoon black pepper

One 17-ounce package puff pastry, thawed

¼ cup Parmesan cheese

1 large egg beaten with 1 tablespoon water, for egg wash

Preheat the oven to 400°F. Line baking sheets with parchment.

Place spinach into a cheesecloth, then wring it out over a sink or bowl to remove as much water as possible. In a large bowl, combine the spinach with the cream cheese, feta cheese, garlic, salt, and pepper. Set aside.

Place the puff pastry onto a lightly floured surface. Use a paring knife to cut out eighteen 3-by-3-inch ovals. Use scraps to add small cat ears onto each one.

Cut additional scraps into 3-inch pieces. Twist, and place alongside the cat heads onto the baking sheet.

Place nine cat head ovals onto the prepped baking sheet. Add a large spoonful of filling into the center of each piece of pastry.

With the remaining nine Flerken-shaped pastry pieces, cut a large hole out of the center to create the mouth. Place these on top of the spinach filling.

Brush all the pastry with the egg wash and sprinkle with Parmesan cheese. Bake for 15 to 17 minutes, until golden brown.

Take the twisted pastry pieces and place into the spinach filling to create the Flerken's mouth tentacles.

Let cool slightly. Serve immediately.

Marvel Studios'
Captain Marvel (2019)

CAPTAIN MARVEL

SKRULL SANDWICHES

Skrulls are capable of mimicking other beings, anyone from a passerby to Nick Fury himself. This recipe invokes the Skrulls' ever-changing nature by dressing jackfruit with brown sugar, cumin, paprika, and cola until it resembles pulled pork. Served on Hawaiian rolls and topped with sweet pickle slices, Skrull Sandwiches prove once again that things aren't always as they appear . . .

V, V+

PREP TIME
10 minutes

COOKING TIME
30 minutes

YIELD
6 servings

DIFFICULTY
Easy

INGREDIENTS

Two 20-ounce cans young green jackfruit, drained

1 tablespoon olive oil

1 large shallot, sliced

2 garlic cloves, minced

3 tablespoons light brown sugar

1 tablespoon cumin

1 tablespoon smoked paprika

1 tablespoon kosher salt

½ teaspoon black pepper

¼ teaspoon cayenne pepper

12 ounces cola

Sweet Hawaiian rolls, for serving

Sweet pickle slices, for serving

Shred the jackfruit by hand. Set aside.

In a skillet over medium-high heat, heat the olive oil. Add the shallot and garlic, cooking for 2 to 3 minutes until softened.

Add the shredded jackfruit, brown sugar, cumin, paprika, salt, pepper, and cayenne, and cook for 2 to 3 minutes, until fragrant. Pour in the cola. Stir to mix, and cook for 5 to 6 minutes until softened and the liquid has cooked down.

Preheat the oven to 400°F. Spread the jackfruit onto a parchment-lined baking sheet. Cook for 20 minutes until fragrant and slightly crispy.

Serve on rolls with sweet pickles.

Marvel Studios' *Captain Marvel* (2019)

CAPTAIN MARVEL PIES

After learning of the Kree's abominable deeds—both to her, and to the entire Skrull race—Carol Danvers decides it's time to change the colors of her Kree Starforce uniform. Opting for a red, blue, and gold flight suit, Carol takes the fight to the Kree. These strawberry and blueberry pies invoke similar shades with a golden crust reminiscent of the eight-pointed star on Captain Marvel's suit. Sweet, buttery, and comforting, these fruit pies are packed with all the energy one needs to go *higher, further, faster*.

V

PREP TIME
20 minutes

COOKING TIME
20 minutes

YIELD
6 pies

DIFFICULTY
Moderate

FOR THE PIE CRUST

1 ½ cups all-purpose flour

¼ teaspoon kosher salt

4 tablespoons unsalted butter

¼ cup vegetable shortening

4 tablespoons ice water

1 large egg white, lightly beaten

FOR THE FILLING

3 cups blueberries

½ cup granulated sugar, divided

4 tablespoons lemon juice, divided

2 tablespoons cornstarch, divided

½ teaspoon cinnamon, divided

½ teaspoon kosher salt, divided

3 cups strawberries, hulled and quartered

6 tablespoons unsalted butter, cut into cubes

1 large egg beaten with 1 tablespoon water, for egg wash

TO MAKE THE PIE CRUST:

In a large bowl whisk together the flour and salt. Add the butter and shortening, working them in together until crumbly. Sprinkle in the water, one tablespoon at a time, working it into the dough until just combined.

Wrap the dough in plastic wrap and chill in the refrigerator for 30 minutes.

Preheat the oven to 350°F. Prep six 5-inch mini pie pans with nonstick spray.

Onto a lightly floured surface, roll out the pie dough. Use an 8-inch round cutter to cut out circles. Press into the mini pie pans, crimping the edges. Prick all over with a fork. Brush with the egg white. Set aside.

TO MAKE THE FILLING:

In a medium bowl, toss the blueberries with ¼ cup of the sugar, 2 tablespoons of the lemon juice, 1 tablespoon of the cornstarch, ¼ teaspoon of the cinnamon, and ¼ teaspoon of the salt. In a second medium bowl, do the same with the strawberries.

Spoon the blueberry mixture into one half of a pie pan and the strawberry mixture into the other half. Repeat with the remaining pie pans. Dot each pie with the diced butter.

On a lightly floured surface, roll out the remaining pie dough. Use a knife to cut out Captain Marvel symbols. Place onto the pies. Brush with egg wash.

Place the pies onto a parchment-lined baking sheet. Bake for 18 to 20 minutes, until golden brown. To prevent the pie tops from sinking, bake separately on a parchment lined baking sheet. Let cool for 10 minutes before serving.

AVENGERS: ENDGAME

THANOS'S SOUP

After snapping his fingers and wiping half the universe out of existence, Thanos takes up residence on a verdant planet where he enjoys a peaceful life on his farm. There, he raises a crop of vegetables, which he harvests to make a nutritious soup. Inspired by Thanos's homegrown meal, this recipe brings together a collection of Terran vegetables intended to invoke the tastes of the Titan's humble garden. With galangal and lemongrass steeped in a tangy broth, this soup is perfectly balanced—as all things should be.

PREP TIME
30 minutes

COOKING TIME
20 minutes

YIELD
4 servings

DIFFICULTY
Moderate

INGREDIENTS

Two 3-inch stalks of lemongrass
5 makrut lime leaves
6 cups water
3-inch galangal root or ginger, peeled and sliced into ¼-inch rounds
2 shallot cloves
1 tomato
2 mini sweet bell peppers
4 teaspoons brown sugar
1 tablespoon shrimp paste in oil
4 teaspoons dried tamarind powder
1 can garbanzo beans
1 carrot, sliced
1 chayote, sliced
½ pound string beans
1 ear corn, quartered
½ head cabbage, roughly chopped
3 teaspoons salt

Smash lemongrass stalks and lime leaves twice using a mortar and pestle to release the flavor.

Add the lemon grass and lime leaves to a large pot. Add the water and bring to a boil.

Turn heat to low.

Using a blender, puree the galangal, shallot cloves, tomato, bell pepper, brown sugar, and dried shrimp paste. Add the tamarind powder to the blended mixture and stir. Add the blended mixture to the pot. Strain the garbanzo beans and add them to the pot. Increase the heat to a boil.

Add the carrot and cook for 3 minutes.

Add the chayote and string beans and cook for 5 minutes.

Add the corn and cook for 3 minutes.

Add the cabbage and cook for 3 minutes.

Add salt to taste and serve.

"I'D ASK WHERE WE WOULD GO ONCE THIS PLAN WAS COMPLETE. HIS ANSWER WAS ALWAYS THE SAME . . . 'TO THE GARDEN.'"

– NEBULA

AVENGERS: ENDGAME

HULK'S BREAKFAST BURRITOS

PREP TIME
30 minutes

COOKING TIME
15 minutes

YIELD
4 normal servings, 1 Hulk-sized serving

DIFFICULTY
Difficult

Once Bruce Banner figures out how to merge his brains with the brawn of the Hulk, he realizes the new, improved, and larger version of himself needs to up his breakfast game. These breakfast burritos are inspired by a meal that Hulk eats with his friends. Eggs, hash browns, and sausages are wrapped in thick, fluffy pancakes to make Super Hero–sized servings. Glazed with maple syrup and best eaten with a big appetite, these breakfast burritos are simultaneously packed with protein and bursting with flavor. They're made from the best of both worlds, just like the reinvigorated Hulk himself.

FOR THE PANCAKES

2 cups all-purpose flour
1 tablespoon light brown sugar
3 tablespoons granulated sugar
1 teaspoon baking powder
½ teaspoon cinnamon
¼ teaspoon kosher salt
1½ cups whole milk
1 large egg, lightly beaten
1 teaspoon vanilla extract
2 tablespoons unsalted butter

FOR THE HASH BROWNS

2 tablespoons unsalted butter
2 cups hash browns
1 teaspoon kosher salt
½ teaspoon onion powder
¼ teaspoon black pepper

FOR THE SCRAMBLE

4 large eggs
2 tablespoons whole milk
½ teaspoon garlic salt
¼ teaspoon white pepper
1 tablespoon olive oil
½ cup diced onion
¼ cup diced red bell pepper
1 garlic clove, minced
4 breakfast sausages, diced
¼ cup maple syrup, for serving

TO MAKE THE PANCAKES:

In a large bowl, whisk the flour, brown sugar, granulated sugar, baking powder, cinnamon, and salt.

Make a well in the center of the dry ingredients. Stir in the milk, egg, and vanilla until just combined.

In a large skillet, over medium heat, melt the butter. Pour ¾ cup batter into the center. Cook for 2 to 3 minutes, until bubbles start to form and pop. Flip over and cook for 1 more minute. Remove from the pan. Repeat with the remaining batter to form four pancakes in total. Set aside on a plate and cover with a tea towel.

TO MAKE THE HASH BROWNS:

Wipe out the same skillet. Over medium-high heat, melt the butter. Add the hash browns and cook for 5 to 6 minutes until browned. Flip over, season with salt, onion powder, and pepper. Cook for 6 to 8 minutes more until browned and crispy. Remove from pan and set aside.

TO MAKE THE SCRAMBLE:

In a large bowl, whisk the eggs, whole milk, garlic salt, and white pepper. Set aside.

In the skillet over medium-high heat, heat the olive oil. Add the onion, bell pepper, and garlic. Cook for 2 to 3 minutes until softened.

Add the breakfast sausages and cook for 2 to 3 minutes until the sausage has browned.

Pour in the egg mixture. Cook, stirring to scramble for 2 to 3 minutes until the eggs have just set.

TO ASSEMBLE THE DISH:

Take a pancake and place it onto a serving plate. Add a spoonful of hashbrowns, then a spoonful of the sausage-egg scramble. Wrap the pancake around the filling, drizzle the maple syrup on top, and serve.

AVENGERS: ENDGAME

NATASHA'S PEANUT BUTTER SANDWICH

The perfect comfort food is tasty, familiar, and oftentimes uncomplicated. When Natasha Romanoff is feeling down, she reaches for a tried-and-true classic—a peanut butter sandwich. This upgraded version pairs peanut butter and bread, but it adds an indulgent twist by adding in some hot honey, bananas, and potato chips. This sandwich might not exactly be conventional, but after one gets emails from a raccoon, nothing sounds crazy anymore.

V

PREP TIME
10 minutes

COOKING TIME
6 minutes

YIELD
1 serving

DIFFICULTY
Easy

INGREDIENTS

3 tablespoons peanut butter

2 slices white bread

1 small banana, peeled and sliced

2 teaspoons hot honey

¼ cup crushed potato chips

1 tablespoon unsalted butter

Spread the peanut butter onto one side of each slice of bread.

Place the bananas onto one slice of the bread. Drizzle the hot honey over the bananas. Add the potato chips. Place the other slice of bread on top, to sandwich.

In a skillet over medium heat, melt the butter. Add the sandwich and cook for 2 to 3 minutes on each side until golden brown.

Slice in half to serve.

"IF YOU'RE ABOUT TO TELL ME TO LOOK ON THE BRIGHT SIDE, I'M ABOUT TO HIT YOU IN THE HEAD WITH A PEANUT BUTTER SANDWICH."

– NATASHA ROMANOFF

Marvel Studios' *Avengers: Endgame* (2019)

ANT-MAN'S TINY TACOS

GF

PREP TIME
20 minutes

COOKING TIME
20 minutes

YIELD
36 mini tacos

DIFFICULTY
Moderate

Scott Lang is just trying to enjoy some tacos on the patio of the Avengers' headquarters when he's hit with a blast of wind as the *Milano* lands nearby. By the time the *Milano* touches down, Scott has lost most of his lunch and some of his dignity. Luckily, Hulk gives Scott two of his own tacos—which of course, look considerably smaller in Hulk's much larger hands. Harkening back to that touching display of friendship, Ant-Man's Tiny Tacos pack ground beef, chorizo, and tasty toppings into miniature versions of crisply fried shells. This crowd-pleasing dish is sure to be enjoyed by heroes of any size.

FOR THE TACO SHELLS

Twelve 6-inch corn tortillas

¼ cup vegetable oil

FOR THE FILLING

1 tablespoon olive oil

½ pound pork chorizo

½ pound ground beef

1 tablespoon chili powder

1 teaspoon cumin

1 teaspoon garlic powder

1 teaspoon onion powder

½ teaspoon paprika

½ teaspoon kosher salt

¼ teaspoon black pepper

FOR THE TOPPINGS

2 cups finely shredded lettuce

1 cup shredded cheddar cheese

1 cup diced tomatoes

½ cup sour cream

TO MAKE THE TACO SHELLS:

Preheat the oven to 375°F. Prep a muffin pan by spraying the bottom side of the pan with nonstick spray.

Microwave the tortillas for 15 seconds, to soften. Use a round cutter to cut 3 small circles out of each tortilla. Brush the circles with oil and place them in between the bottom pan sections to form taco shapes.

Bake for 5 to 7 minutes, until crispy. Leave in the pan and set aside.

TO MAKE THE FILLING:

In a large skillet over medium-high heat, heat the olive oil. Add the chorizo and ground beef and cook for 8 minutes, until meat is browned. Season with chili powder, cumin, garlic powder, onion powder, paprika, salt, and black pepper. Cook for 2 minutes more.

TO ASSEMBLE THE TOPPINGS:

Spoon the meat into the taco shells. Top with lettuce, cheese, and tomatoes. Add sour cream to serve.

AVENGERS: ENDGAME

SAUERKRAUT SLIDERS

In *Avengers: Endgame*, Tony Stark has the chance to speak with a younger version of his father. As they chat, he learns that Howard is bringing a can of sauerkraut (and a bouquet of flowers) home to his pregnant wife. Sauerkraut Sliders combine the classic sandwich topping with pastrami, pickles, and Swiss cheese in a flavorful burst of Stark-inspired goodness. Doused with Thousand Island Dressing and served on marble rye, this dish is sure to satisfy any craving—past, present, or future.

PREP TIME
15 minutes

COOKING TIME
5 minutes

YIELD
16 servings

DIFFICULTY
Easy

INGREDIENTS

6 tablespoons unsalted butter, softened

8 slices marble rye

1 cup Thousand Island dressing

12 slices pastrami

1 cup sauerkraut, well drained

8 slices Swiss cheese

16 pickle slices

Preheat the oven to 400°F.

Spread the butter onto one side of each slice of bread. Place four slices of bread, buttered side down, onto the prepped baking sheet.

Spread half the Thousand Island dressing onto the bread.

Top each bread slice with pickle slices, pastrami, then the sauerkraut.

Drizzle the remaining Thousand Island dressing on top.

Add the cheese.

Top with the remaining bread, buttered side up.

Bake for 3 to 5 minutes until browned.

Cut each sandwich into four pieces to serve.

"FLOWERS AND SAUERKRAUT, YOU GOT A BIG DATE TONIGHT?"

– TONY STARK

"NO, MY WIFE'S EXPECTING. AND, UH, TOO MUCH TIME AT THE OFFICE."

– HOWARD STARK

SPIDER-MAN: FAR FROM HOME

"PETER TINGLE" BANANA MUFFINS

V

PREP TIME
20 minutes

COOKING TIME
20 minutes

YIELD
12 muffins

DIFFICULTY
Easy

Spider-Man is known for his incredible intuition, which May affectionately refers to as his "Peter Tingle" . . . and when he fails to dodge the banana she tosses his way, she wonders exactly *how* his extra sense works. Peter might find his aunt's choice of words epically embarrassing, but he'd be sure to approve of their namesake baked bounty. Topped with cinnamon and sugar and dusted with walnuts, "Peter Tingle" Banana Muffins are a light, fluffy banana-seasoned treat. They're great to bring on picnics, lunches, or even class trips . . . just so long as you have a tingle about it!

FOR THE MUFFINS

2 cups all-purpose flour

½ cup granulated sugar

¼ cup light brown sugar

1½ teaspoons baking powder

½ teaspoon ground cinnamon

¼ teaspoon kosher salt

3 large ripe bananas, mashed

2 large eggs

6 tablespoons unsalted butter, melted

1 tablespoon honey

1 teaspoon vanilla extract

FOR THE TOPPING

2 tablespoons cold unsalted butter, diced

½ cup packed light brown sugar

¼ cup all-purpose flour

1 teaspoon ground cinnamon

½ cup diced walnuts

TO MAKE THE MUFFINS:

Preheat the oven to 375°F. Prep a muffin pan with liners.

In a large bowl, whisk the flour, granulated sugar, brown sugar, baking powder, cinnamon, and salt. Set aside.

Make a well in the center of the dry ingredients, stir in the mashed bananas, eggs, butter, honey, and vanilla until just combined.

Spoon the batter into the prepped muffin pan.

TO MAKE THE TOPPING:

For the topping, in a small bowl, cut the butter into the brown sugar, flour, and cinnamon until crumbly. Stir in the walnuts. Sprinkle onto the muffin batter.

Bake for 17 to 20 minutes until an inserted toothpick comes out clean. Let cool on a wire rack.

"I THOUGHT THAT YOU COULD SENSE THAT WITH YOUR . . . PETER TINGLE."

– MAY PARKER

"PLEASE DO NOT START CALLING IT MY PETER TINGLE!"

– PETER PARKER

"SO WHAT'S UP? YOU CAN DODGE BULLETS BUT NOT BANANAS?"

– MAY PARKER

MERINGUE KISSES

Between attending classes at Midtown School of Science and Technology and saving the world as Spider-Man, Peter Parker's schedule is packed. But when he heads to Europe on his class trip, the only thing he wants to do is relax with his friends and *finally* share his feelings for M.J. at the top of the Eiffel Tower. Yet, as is often the case, Peter's double life gets in the way. Meringue kisses, a dessert that originated in France, are a sweet way to honor Peter's thwarted plans. These treats are sweet and airy, and while they might not be what Peter was looking for, they make it easier to be so far from home.

GF, V

PREP TIME
2 hours, 15 minutes

COOKING TIME
3 hours

YIELD
60 cookies

DIFFICULTY
Moderate

INGREDIENTS

2 large egg whites, at room temperature

¼ teaspoon cream of tartar

½ cup confectioners' sugar

½ teaspoon vanilla extract

Pink food coloring

Preheat the oven to 200°F. Prep baking sheets with parchment.

In the bowl of an electric mixer, add the egg whites and cream of tartar. Whip until foamy.

Slowly add the confectioners' sugar while continuing to whip until stiff peaks have formed. Fold in the vanilla and pink food coloring.

Transfer the mixture into a large pastry bag fitted with a jumbo star tip. Pipe 1-inch diameter meringues onto the prepped sheets.

Bake for 1 hour, until the meringues are dry. Turn the oven off and leave the pan in the oven with the door closed for another 2 hours.

Remove from parchment to serve.

Marvel Studios' *Spider-Man: Far From Home* (2019)

SPIDER-MAN: FAR FROM HOME

MYSTERIO'S MATCHA

In his vibrant emerald suit, Mysterio, the would-be Super Hero and master of illusion, is instantly recognizable. But maintaining appearances can be exhausting, and this refreshing recipe would be just what any scheming charlatan would need to re-energize. Here, iced matcha is topped with a round scoop of ice cream, molded to mimic the shape of the faux hero's helmet. Sharp, sweet, and just the slightest bit nutty, this drink evokes the spirit of Mysterio himself.

GF, V

PREP TIME
10 minutes

COOKING TIME
N/A

YIELD
1 serving

DIFFICULTY
Easy

INGREDIENTS

¼ cup oat milk

1 tablespoon granulated sugar

1 teaspoon matcha powder, sifted

¼ teaspoon vanilla extract

1 cup ice

1 cup coconut milk

1 scoop matcha ice cream

In a small glass, whisk the oat milk, sugar, matcha powder, and vanilla for 2 to 3 minutes until the sugar dissolves. Set aside.

Fill a tall glass with ice. Pour in the coconut milk, then the matcha mixture. Add the scoop of matcha ice cream on top to serve.

Marvel Studios' *Spider-Man: Far From Home* (2019)

DIETARY CONSIDERATIONS

PHASE ONE	V	V+	GF
"I Am Iron Man" Cheeseburger			
Proof that Tony Stark Has a Tart	●		
Smashed Potatoes	●		●
Undercover Pizza	●		
Giant Donut	●		
Strawberry Roses	●		●
Smoked Salmon Carpaccio			●
Watermelon Blast	●		●
Worthy Chops			
Asgardian Squash Soup	●	●	●
"Another!" Coffee	●		●
Cap's Shield Cookies	●		
Capsicles	●	●	●
Stark Expo Treats	●		
Chocolate-Covered Blueberries	●		●
Team Shawarma			
The Space Scone	●		

PHASE TWO	V	V+	GF
Harley's Baked Potatoes			●
Gluten-Free Waffles	●		●
Nine Realms Stew	●	●	●
Sif's Sliced Salad	●		●
The Reality Scone	●		
Chicken Satay			●
Red Wings			●
"I Am Groot" Breadsticks	●		
What a Bunch of Donut Holes	●		
The Power Scone	●		
Asgardian Ale	●	●	●
Pietro's Speedy Eggs	●		●
The Mind Scone	●		
Ant-Sized Tea Cookies	●		
The Sundae of Omnipotence	●		
Pym Particle Bites			●

PHASE THREE	V	V+	GF
Wanda's Paprikash			
Does Anyone Have Any Orange Sorbet?	●	●	●
May's Walnut Date Loaf	●		
Eggs of Agamatto	●		
The Time Scone	●		
Roasted Yaro Root	●	●	●
Trash Panda Cookies	●		
Celestials Parfait			●
Ravager Salute Cupcakes	●		
Peter's Bodega Sandwich			
Larby Larb			●
Spidey Churro Bites	●		
Grandmaster's Melty Grilled Cheese	●		
Valkyrie's Pegasus Punch	●	●	●
The Cupcake of Champions	●		

PHASE THREE	V	V+	GF
Heart-Shaped Herb Lemonade	●		●
Shuri's Bhajias	●	●	
River Tribe Tilapia with Efo Riro			
West African Fried Chicken and Plantain Waffles			
The Dora Milaje's Pilau			●
Border Tribe Lemon Chicken			●
Jabari Tribe Peanut Stew	●	●	●
Stark Raving Hazelnuts	●	●	●
Wong's Favorite Hulk-Inspired Fudge Ice Cream	●		
Wong's Tuna Melt			
The Soul Scone	●		
Infinitea	●	●	●
X-Con Fancy Pastries	●		
Jimmy Woo's Magic Noodles			
San Francisco Clam Chowder			
Truth Serum	●	●	●
Diagonally Cut French Toast	●		
Flerken Nibbles	●		
Skrull Sandwiches	●	●	
Captain Marvel Pies	●		
Thanos's Soup			
Hulk's Breakfast Burritos			
Natasha's Peanut Butter Sandwich	●		
Ant-Man's Tiny Tacos			●
Sauerkraut Sliders			
"Peter Tingle" Banana Muffins	●		
Meringue Kisses	●		●
Mysterio's Matcha	●		●

POST CREDITS	V	V+	GF
Miss Minute Cookies	●		
Mobius Salad Variants: Variant 1	●		●
Mobius Salad Variants: Variant 2	●	●	●
Mobius Salad Variants: Variant 3	●	●	●

MEASUREMENT CONVERSIONS

VOLUME

US	METRIC
⅕ teaspoon (tsp)	1 mL
1 teaspoon (tsp)	5 mL
1 tablespoon (tbsp)	15 mL
1 fluid ounce (fl. oz.)	30 mL
1/5 cup	50 mL
¼ cup	60 mL
⅓ cup	80 mL
3.4 fluid ounces (fl. oz.)	100 mL
½ cup	120 mL
⅔ cup	160 mL
¾ cup	180 mL
1 cup	240 mL
1 pint (2 cups)	480 mL
1 quart (4 cups)	.95 liter

WEIGHT

OUNCES	GRAMS
.5 ounce (oz.)	14 grams (g)
1 ounce (oz.)	28 grams (g)
¼ pound (lb.)	113 grams (g)
⅓ pound (lb.)	151 grams (g)
½ pound (lb.)	227 grams (g)
1 pound (lb.)	454 grams (g)

TEMPERATURES

FAHRENHEIT	CELSIUS
200°F	93°C
212°F	100°C
250°F	121°C
275°F	135°C
300°F	149°C
325°F	163°C
350°F	177°C
400°F	204°C
425°F	218°C
450°F	232°C
475°F	246°C
500°F	260°C

ABOUT THE AUTHORS

JENN FUJIKAWA is a lifestyle and pop culture author, content creator, and host. She has created content for Lucasfilm, Marvel, Disney, and more. Jenn is the author of multiple fandom-based cookbooks including *Star Wars: The Life Day Cookbook*, *Star Wars: The Padawan Cookbook*, *Ghostbusters: The Official Cookbook*, *Parks and Recreation: The Official Cookbook*, *The Princess Bride: The Official Cookbook*, and many more. For more of her recipes check out her Instagram at @justjennrecipes.

S. T. BENDE is a young-adult and children's author, known for the Norse mythology series Viking Academy and the Ære Saga. She's also written books for Disney, Lucasfilm, Pixar, The Jim Henson Company, and Marvel. She lives on the West Coast, where she spends far too much time at Disneyland, and she dreams of skiing on Jotunheim and Hoth. www.stbende.com.

EVI AKI—a passionate home cook and food blogger based in Los Angeles—established *Ev's Eats* in 2016. Her blog quickly gained recognition for its flavor-filled recipes and user-friendly cooking advice. Evi's authentic love for food shines through in every dish she creates, fueling her journey to curate innovative recipes and content.

Evi's work has been featured in prestigious publications and platforms, such as *Food 52, Essence Magazine*, *The Washington Post*, and *BuzzFeed.* Additionally, she is the author of *Flavors of Africa: Discover Authentic Family Recipes from All Over the Continent*, a testament to her dedication to celebrating diverse flavors and cultures through food.

ACKNOWLEDGMENTS

To the Fantastic Four in my life: Alice Kawakami; Kyle, Tyler, and Mason Fujikawa; and Mark Kawakami. To my very own Revengers: Mel Caylo, Cheryl deCarvalho, Chrissy Dinh, Chrys Hasegawa, Sarah Kuhn, and Robb Pearlman. To S.T. Bende, thank you for guarding this galaxy with me. To Harrison Tunggal, Emma Merwin, and Tim Pilcher, thank you for being the Watchers of this book universe. Finally, to my kids, I love you 3000.

JENN FUJIKAWA

A hero-sized *thank you* to Marvel for letting me play in your Universe. To Jenn Fujikawa—I will love your cookbooks 'Til the End Of The Line, and this one has been a thrill to create with you! To my Friends from Work, Harrison Tunggal, Emma Merwin, Sammy Holland, and Tim Pilcher—thank you for keeping our Quinjet airborne. To Earth's Wizards and my personal superheroes, the Imagineers—thank you for creating Avengers Campus. (And to my husband, who happily stood in line well before the sun came up on opening day—You Are Worthy!) And of course, to my very own Ironman and Thor: I love you. For All Time, Always.

S. T. BENDE

Crafting these recipes has been a love-filled journey, celebrating diverse flavors and cultures in the African diaspora. Thanks to my family's unwavering support, especially to my culinary muse, my mom, whose love shapes every dish. To my vibrant blog community, readers, and adventurous friends, your enthusiasm fuels my creativity. Special thanks to Orezi & Oreva for being my culinary co-adventurers. These recipes are a celebration of diversity and the power of food to unite. With heartfelt gratitude, this book is dedicated to all who've joined me in this flavorful adventure. Love, Evi Aki.

EVI AKI

INDEX

D

E

F

G

H

I

J

K

L

T

U

V

W

X

Y

POST-CREDITS RECIPES

As any true believer knows, it's always worth it to stick around after the credits to get a sneak peek at the future of the Marvel Cinematic Universe—or in this case, a teaser for meals that will span the Multiverse. Your culinary adventures are far from over . . .

The aftermath of *Avengers: Endgame* may have left our heroes heartbroken and Marvel's Cinematic Universe void of some of its most beloved Avengers. But new heroes are out there, ready to step in to join Earth's Mightiest in avenging our planet and guarding the galaxy. Perhaps new recipes await us too—whether inspired by Shang Chi's unique upbringing (and unparalleled parking skills) or Ant-Man and the Wasp's quandaries within the Quantum Realm. After all, the MCU doesn't end with *Endgame*.

MISS MINUTES COOKIES

As the aggressively cheerful greeter of the Time Variance Authority (or TVA for short), Miss Minutes is tasked with orienting the agency's new arrivals. Loki finds her presence to be anything but soothing, but even the incarcerated God of Mischief would appreciate this cookie variant of the famed Miss Minutes. Sugar, flour, and eggs are baked into rounds, then decorated with the upbeat smile and sparkling eyes of the TVA's animated mascot. Miss Minutes Cookies are so delightful, you'll want to enjoy them for all time. Always.

V

PREP TIME
45 minutes

COOKING TIME
10 minutes

YIELD
18 cookies

DIFFICULTY
Difficult

FOR THE COOKIES

3 cups all-purpose flour
1 teaspoon baking powder
½ teaspoon cinnamon
¼ teaspoon nutmeg
¼ teaspoon kosher salt
1 cup unsalted butter, softened
½ cup light brown sugar
½ cup granulated sugar
1 large egg
½ teaspoon almond extract
½ teaspoon vanilla extract

FOR THE FROSTING

5 cups confectioners' sugar
3 tablespoons meringue powder
6 tablespoons whole milk
½ teaspoon clear vanilla extract
2 to 3 drops orange food drops coloring
2 ounces black icing
2 ounces white icing

TO MAKE THE COOKIES:

In a medium bowl, whisk together the flour, baking powder, cinnamon, nutmeg, and salt. Set aside.

In the bowl of an electric mixer, cream the butter, brown sugar, and granulated sugar until fluffy.

Stir in the egg, almond extract, and vanilla extract until just combined.

Slowly add in the dry ingredients, until the dough just comes together. Divide into two and wrap in plastic wrap. Refrigerate until you are ready to use.

Preheat the oven to 350°F. Prep baking sheets with parchment paper.

Roll out the dough ¼ inch thick. Use a 3½ inch-round cutter to cut out circles or a paper Miss Minutes template to cut cookies to shape. Transfer onto the prepped baking sheets.

Bake for 10 minutes. Let cool on a wire rack.

TO MAKE THE FROSTING:

In the bowl of an electric mixer, stir together the confectioners' sugar and the meringue powder. Slowly add the milk and clear vanilla until the icing comes together. Stir in the orange food coloring.

Pipe the orange frosting around the edge of the cookie. Flood the center with frosting and let set.

Once the orange frosting is dry, use the black and white icings to create the rest of the face details. When the icing is dry, the cookies are ready to serve.

Marvel Studios' *Loki* (2021)

MOBIUS SALAD VARIANTS

VARIANT 1: CORN SALAD

It's Mobius' job at the TVA to cull variants, but he might have second thoughts about cutting any one of these three salad variants, including an esquites-inspired corn dish, some refreshing cucumbers, and brightly colored carrots. Any way they're sliced, each of these salads is sure to serve up their own glorious purpose. The Timekeepers wouldn't have it any other way.

GF, V

PREP TIME
15 minutes

COOKING TIME
45 minutes

YIELD
6 servings

DIFFICULTY
Moderate

INGREDIENTS

6 ears corn, in their husks
2 tablespoons unsalted butter
½ teaspoon seasoned salt
⅓ cup torn cilantro
½ teaspoon chili powder
¼ cup crumbled Cotija cheese
1 green onion, diced
Lime wedges, for serving

Preheat the oven to 375°F. Place the corn directly onto the oven rack. Cook for 45 minutes. Remove and let cool slightly.

Husk the corn, removing and discarding the silk. Hold the corn vertically and use a sharp knife to cut the kernels off each cob.

Place the kernels into a large bowl with the butter and seasoned salt. Toss to coat, until the butter has melted. Fold in the cilantro.

Sprinkle with chili powder and Cotija cheese.

Add the green onion and lime wedges, to serve.

"LET'S JUST SAY YOUR SALAD IS ASGARD IN THIS SCENARIO."

– LOKI

"NO. IT'S NOT ASGARD. THAT'S MY LUNCH."

– MOBIUS

MOBIUS SALAD VARIANTS

VARIANT 2: CUCUMBER SALAD

GF, V, V+

PREP TIME
25 minutes

COOKING TIME
N/A

YIELD
4 servings

DIFFICULTY
Easy

INGREDIENTS

2 cups cucumbers, peeled and diced

1 teaspoon kosher salt

1 shallot, peeled and thinly sliced

1 tablespoon tamari

1 tablespoon mirin (sweet rice wine)

1 tablespoon light brown sugar

½ teaspoon shichimi togarashi (Japanese spice blend)

1 teaspoon black sesame seeds

2 green onions, diced

In a colander over a medium bowl, toss the cucumbers with the salt. Let sit for 20 minutes to drain. Rinse.

Transfer the drained cucumbers to a medium serving bowl. Toss with the sliced shallot, tamari, mirin, and brown sugar.

Sprinkle with shichimi togarashi, sesame seeds, and green onions to serve.

Marvel Studios' *Loki* (2021)

MOBIUS SALAD VARIANTS

VARIANT 3: CARROT SALAD

GF, V, V+

PREP TIME
10 minutes

COOKING TIME
N/A

YIELD
4 servings

DIFFICULTY
Easy

FOR THE DRESSING

2 tablespoons vegetable oil

2 tablespoons tamari

1 tablespoon granulated sugar

2 teaspoons rice vinegar

1 teaspoon sesame oil

1 clove garlic, minced

½ teaspoon pressed fresh ginger

FOR THE SALAD

1½ cups shredded carrots

2 tablespoons chopped fresh cilantro

2 tablespoons chopped fresh parsley

2 green onions, diced

1 teaspoon toasted sesame seeds

TO MAKE THE DRESSING:

In a small jar with a lid, combine the oil, tamari, sugar, rice vinegar, sesame oil, garlic, and ginger. Put the lid on the jar, and shake well until the sugar has dissolved. Set aside.

TO MAKE THE SALAD:

In a medium bowl, toss the carrots, cilantro, parsley, and green onion. Drizzle the dressing over the salad, toss to coat.

Sprinkle with sesame seeds to serve.

Marvel Studios' *Loki* (2021)

INSIGHT EDITIONS

PO Box 3088
San Rafael, CA 94912
www.insighteditions.com

Find us on Facebook: www.facebook.com/InsightEditions
Follow us on Instagram: @insighteditions

MARVEL

ISBN: 979-8-88663-541-6

Publisher: Raoul Goff
VP, Group Publisher: Vanessa Lopez
VP, Manufacturing: Alix Nicholaeff
Associate Publisher: Thom O'Hearn
Art Director: Stuart Smith
Senior Designer: Brooke McCullum
Executive Editor: Anja Schmidt
Associate Editor: Emma Merwin
Executive Managing Editor: Maria Spano
Managing Editor: Shannon Ballesteros
Production Editor: Ivy Long
Production Manager: Deena Hashem
Strategic Production Planner, Subsidiary Rights: Lina s Palma-Temena

Photography by Lindsay Kreighbaum
Drink and Food Styling by Bianca Swanepoel
Prop Styling by Aimie Vredevoogd

MARVEL STUDIOS THE INFINITY SAGA

All titles now streaming on Disney+.

MARVEL PUBLISHING
Jeff Youngquist, VP, Production and Special Projects
Sarah Singer, Editor, Special Projects
Jeremy West, Manager, Licensed Publishing
Sven Larsen, VP, Business Development and Licensed Publishing
David Gabriel, VP, Comic Sales and Content Planning
C.B. Cebulski, Editor in Chief

MARVEL STUDIOS
President: Kevin Feige
Co-President: Louis D'Esposito
VP, Franchise Creative & Marketing: Sarah Truly Beers
Director, Franchise & Marketing: Kristy Amornkul
Franchise Story Team: Jacqueline Ryan-Rudolph, Kyle Quigley, Kandon Haynes
Manager, Marvel Archives: Tamarin Panama
Associate Principal Counsel: Nigel Goodwin
Director, Clearances: Erika Denton
Manager, Clearances: Jennifer Wojnar
Director, Credits: Jeff Willis
Manager, Credits: Jennifer Giandalone
Licensing Specialist: Vincent Garcia

ROOTS of PEACE   REPLANTED PAPER

Insight Editions, in association with Roots of Peace, will plant two trees for each tree used in the manufacturing of this book. Roots of Peace is an internationally renowned humanitarian organization dedicated to eradicating land mines worldwide and converting war-torn lands into productive farms and wildlife habitats. Roots of Peace will plant two million fruit and nut trees in Afghanistan and provide farmers there with the skills and support necessary for sustainable land use.

Manufactured in China by Insight Editions

10 9 8 7 6 5 4 3 2 1